Reading with Writing in Mind

Praise for *Reading with Writing in Mind*

"This book reminds us that building students' literacy skills can and must be done by educators in every discipline. By including many specific strategies and real classroom examples, Charron, Fenton, and Harris provide all teachers with resources needed to integrate the teaching of literacy in any content area."—**Dr. Susan Szachowicz, Senior Fellow, International Center for Leadership in Education**

"This text is an immensely useful and enlivening overview of techniques and tools that teachers in all content areas will find useful in doing their disciplinary work. The unique contribution of this book is the promotion of wide-awake reading in service of developing competent and reflective writers of all kinds of texts. The approach starts with the foregrounding of purpose, and is highly motivating and assistive in ways that will transform teacher practice, but even more importantly, that will transform student attitudes, engagement, and achievement."—**Jeffrey D. Wilhelm, Distinguished Professor of English Education at Boise State University and author,** *Engaging Readers and Writers with Inquiry*

Reading with Writing in Mind

A Guide for Middle and High School Educators

Nancy Charron
Marilyn Fenton
Margaret Harris

ROWMAN & LITTLEFIELD
Lanham • Boulder • New York • London

Published by Rowman & Littlefield
A wholly owned subsidiary of The Rowman & Littlefield Publishing Group, Inc.
4501 Forbes Boulevard, Suite 200, Lanham, Maryland 20706
www.rowman.com

Unit A, Whitacre Mews, 26-34 Stannary Street, London SE11 4AB

British Library Cataloguing in Publication Information Available

Library of Congress Cataloging-in-Publication Data Available

ISBN 9781475840049 (hardback : alk. paper) | ISBN 9781475840056 (pbk. : alk. paper) | ISBN 9781475840063 (electronic)

♾™ The paper used in this publication meets the minimum requirements of American National Standard for Information Sciences—Permanence of Paper for Printed Library Materials, ANSI/NISO Z39.48-1992.

Printed in the United States of America

Contents

Preface

This book addresses the need for all content area teachers, in addition to English language arts teachers, to become effective teachers of literacy.

WHAT MAKES THIS BOOK UNIQUE?

This book meets the needs of the school district and the individual teacher by providing the rationale and activities that increase students' literacy skills. These activities have been used in real classroom settings by the authors. Students in all content areas are faced with the challenge of reading texts. Teachers can use these readings as well as their own content readings to enhance students' reading *and* writing skills.

It offers background information and gives reasons as to why and how various literacy practices are effective. In addition, a variety of activities are aligned with the Common Core Standards. Relevant reading and writing standards preface each chapter's activities. A student learning objective and a statement of how and why the activity improves reading and writing skills also precedes each activity. At the end of each activity, a suggestion for assessment is offered. All activities follow a Universal Design for Learning protocol. Our objective is to help teachers reach *all* their students by offering an array of motivating and flexible strategies and activities.

For students with moderate to severe special needs, English Language Learners, and/or low-performing students, text boxes are provided giving adaptation ideas. With an emphasis on research-based practices and on effective implementation, there will be improvement in access in all content areas for all students.

USING THIS BOOK

This book offers school professional learning teams the opportunity to do a "book study" in a whole-group format. Now all middle school and secondary school teachers (grades 6 to 12) are responsible for promoting literacy. This book offers them a wonderful opportunity to learn and implement reading strategies that enhance students' writing across the curriculum. It may also be used in universities or colleges in teacher preparation programs.

Introduction

> If you would be a writer, first be a reader. Only through the assimilation of ideas, thoughts, and philosophies can one begin to focus his own ideas, thoughts, and philosophies.
>
> —Allan W. Eckert

At the end of 12 years of schooling, students should graduate high school ready for the world of college and/or work. Statistics show, however, that about 40 percent of college freshmen are deficient in their writing skills and must take a remedial course before they take a college composition course (ACT, 2011). These students are truly at a disadvantage. To be successful in their college courses and in life in general, they need to write proficiently. Yet no one can write well without being a student of text.

Words shape both the medium and the message. Without words, a writer has no paint to paint, no pencil to draw, and no movement to dance. From what does the power derive? The answer depends on the skill of the writer in choosing words and arranging them not only for meaning but also for both effect and affect. Good writing informs, persuades, and inspires!

To become a competent writer, one must gain control of one's words and ideas. To learn to write well, students will benefit from studying excellent writing more closely and building a bridge between reading and writing. Why is some writing "great"? Great writers make choices that a budding writer could also make. Good writers are proficient readers who know how to lead their reader through the text.

The greatest barrier to being a successful student writer is the inability to read between the lines and place a piece of writing into the broader context. If a reader cannot discern the attitude of the writer, a skill well beyond reading for surface meaning, then the real intent of the writer or the deeper meaning of the text may well be lost. As Stephen King (2000) states in his book *On Writing*, "The real importance of reading is that it creates an ease and intimacy with the process of writing; one comes to the country of the writer with one's papers and identification pretty much in order. Constant reading will pull you into a place (a mind-set, if you like the phrase) where you can write eagerly and without self-consciousness" (p. 150).

Many students will readily admit that they have not chosen to spend much time reading and that there are other, more "fun" things to do. So, if one wishes to be successful, how exactly does one make up for years of *not reading* or reading for simple comprehension without discernment? In order to foster truly competent writers, it is imperative that teachers instruct students to take the time to notice what good writers do to engage a reader. Teaching students to notice the construction of a written piece is an integral part of the Common Core Standards.

How can teachers instruct students to become discerning readers? In fact, many practices that build close reading skills (Fisher & Frey, 2014) can be adapted from the early grades, with any student of any age or level. It is as simple as stopping to notice the details in a picture or a word that tickles or impresses in the way it is used. It can be as easy as asking what the difference is between shorter sentences and longer sentences in storytelling. What is the effect of having so much white space on a page? A good writer is first a good reader. A good reader notices everything. This is a skill for all disciplines at all stages of learning.

This book is concerned with providing a rationale and an array of tested activities that will foster good writing through better reading. All the authors are experienced teachers who now apply that expertise to college students in teacher preparation programs. All are former public school teachers, one in high school English, one in high school social studies, and one in special education and literacy. Every activity has been used and personally tested by the authors in actual school classrooms.

Each of us has left a mark on every chapter. Chapter 1 finds its roots in the language arts curriculum. Chapter 2 takes that framework and adapts the ideas for content area reading and writing. Chapters 3 and 4 examine the uses and protocols of various forms of essay writing. It has been noted that every genre or purpose is, in a sense, persuasive in that the writer seeks to bring a reader to his or her perspective, whether the subject is science, history, or the analysis of literature. These chapters are key in achieving the learning goals of the Common Core Standards. It is essential to the citizen to recognize how reading influences our minds and how to wield words for a purpose. Chapter 5, on poetry, also holds powerful lessons for the young writer.

The chapters on reading and writing in a genre are not meant to be instructional texts for writing essays or poems. Rather, the purpose of these chapters is to help all prospective writers raise their general literacy skills and recognize that creativity is not outside the realm of possibility despite the discipline imposed by each subject by its favored forms and conventions. Converting a narrative to a personal essay teaches a student how to harness the power of an idea. Incorporating poetic elements into prose helps underscore the amazing variety of choices in our language available to a well-read writer.

Chapter 6 addresses an overarching principle of our book: that Universal Design for Learning techniques can provide access to all students. Chapter 7 asks writers to apply their best reading techniques in critiquing and editing their own writing. Chapter 8 concludes the book in addressing the closing of the "literacy loop."

The ideas presented have been designed to motivate and include all learners. The teacher's role is to make available to the entire class choices and adaptations and to allow those students who will benefit the opportunity to use them. To ensure success for everyone, teachers let all learners know *why* it is important to understand particular concepts and provide each of them with the instructional path they require to be successful. For those students who require *extensive* accommodations, ideas are provided in text boxes throughout the book.

Most reading in our everyday lives is directly tied to a practical purpose, and we cannot take informational text for granted. So-called technical writing belongs with its subject area, and the academic language developed in each field requires instruction. No longer should science or social studies teachers insist that they cannot teach reading and writing skills to their students. Teachers who share the literacy standards and incorporate them into the reading and writing tasks embedded in their subject will be more likely to support one another's efforts to meet their students' needs in a more cohesive curriculum.

A chemistry teacher who insists that science deals only with facts and so doesn't infuse opinion into what is published or read is limiting the knowledge base of the students. Every science article includes and excludes data by the choice of the researcher or writer. Every science reader and every reader of history is vulnerable if he or she cannot recognize how to read nonfiction texts for tone as well as for information. The Common Core Literacy Anchor Standards cited in the various activities are adaptable and can be made applicable to the reading and writing tasks in various content areas.

All people, no matter the field or the job, benefit from the ability to explain themselves and engage in both oral and written advocacy for themselves and their ideas. The Common Core's approach to literacy effectively addresses this need by distributing the reading and writing tasks across the curriculum.

The Common Core Standards also provide continuity to those student populations who move frequently. For example, students may live with a parent in one town for part of a school year and then live with a parent in another town for the remainder of the school year. The migrant student population often suffers from having an inconsistent curriculum. Having Common Core Standards provides these student populations stability in the curriculum from school district to school district.

It is never too early or too late for any student to build stronger literacy skills. One can learn to read with more discernment by picking up a pen or turning on a computer and composing lines that are meaningful or important to him or her. Conversely, one can learn to write better through more and better reading. Reading and writing are not only complementary; they are symbiotic. Thus, this book about teaching writers begins with a chapter titled "Reading to Improve Student Writing."

1

Reading to Improve Student Writing

> Reading is practice for a writer in the same way that time at the piano is practice for the pianist.
>
> —Amy McNamara

It is surprising, even shocking, how many students manage to spend 12 years in school without understanding why they should read. And it is all too easy to find students who say they don't read and even "hate to read." Students in college (even prospective teachers!) report that they loved to read in elementary school but that, beginning with middle school, they stopped seeking out reading for pleasure and then found ways to resist having to read, often right through high school.

What have we done to kill their early positive attitudes? Chris Tovani (2000), in her book about reawakening a love of reading in our students, writes about "fake reading" and other ways in which teachers—wanting the best for their students— are hoodwinked by clever and resistant students. Kelly Gallagher (2011) identifies choice as a motivational tool, encouraging his ninth graders to choose a book they want to read and then providing some class time for them to "dig in." He also advocates deliberate building of informational background through reading and classroom discussion, adding nonfiction and informational reading to English class. We educators should use these ideas and expand our options to promote the "love of the word" among our students.

CELEBRATING LANGUAGE

It is clear that educators need to inspire and motivate if they want students to have some enthusiasm about their reading. From the start of class in September, teachers

1

need to make it clear that language is loved and celebrated and varies across cultures. Every family has a distinctive vocabulary reflecting their cultural backgrounds and interests. Invite students to collect words and phrases they like to share with the class. Stop class to take time to admire a word choice or a bit of interesting imagery. Collect academic vocabulary so that you can share understanding in a specific content area.

In English class, collect words to discuss grammar and writing, literature, poetry, newly coined words (neologisms), and anything else that pleases. In social studies, collect geographical terms, terms for systems of government, historical time periods, and sociological and psychological terms. Every subject and field has its own collection of useful words. Celebrate all because the broader the vocabulary, the more tools we have.

Encourage and motivate with words. Make their study a party rather than a chore. Require the core list for class and then let them add a few of their own. A fun way to collect words is by using wordles (http://www.wordle.net), having students build word banks related to their reading, and allowing the technology to create artistic displays of these words. Once they have a practical wordle built and displayed, they may use those words in whatever content area the reading relates to or perhaps across content areas—for example, in social studies, perhaps an essay explaining a historical event; in science, perhaps using the wordle to explain a scientific process; or in mathematics, using the wordle to illustrate an application. In other words, connect the wordle to the specific content.

CLOSE READING: NOTICING THE WRITER'S CHOICES

In every subject, teachers can actively point out effective writing to their students. Let's not settle for basic comprehension. In the middle of reading a novel or a poem (or a speech or a letter), we can stop to graze. What does the writer want the reader to feel? How can we tell? Once students identify meaningful and effective features in what they read, they can begin to implement those features in their own writing.

Middle and high school classes spend a fair amount of time talking and writing about their reading. By the time they are in high school, many students have developed some modest skills in this regard, and they will be able to express their ideas and opinions about literature, arguing a point of view. Often, the most adept readers commandeer the discussion, leaving the rest of the class out. Or discussions are had at the top class levels in a homogeneously grouped school, leaving the less adept readers to struggle with less rigorous content.

Yet all students can be invited to capture their thoughts and ideas in writing before a discussion is launched so that every student has an answer ready and can contribute. If some students need additional support to participate in a higher-level discussion, they may take three to five minutes to write out their thoughts and then share them with another student prior to discussion. They might receive the question the day before class for extra processing time. Or they could review the question ahead of time in a "study skills" or "directed study" class. Having tested the idea with another person, the student gains clarity and confidence. Students learn the value of writing down their thoughts. They also learn the process of conferring with a peer or other helpful person to try out their ideas and expressions.

CLOSE READING REVEALS THE WRITER'S ATTITUDE

Close reading, as stated in the Common Core Anchor Reading Standards, is a skill that facilitates reading comprehension in all content areas. Fisher and Frey (2014) point out that repeated readings increase deeper understanding of text. By frequently discussing and writing about the choices a writer has made in crafting the text, students can improve their own toolbox of literacy skills (Levine, 2014). Either the teacher or the student can choose a short passage, a paragraph, or a page from what they are reading and notice how it is put together. They seek to answer the question, *How does the form support the meaning?*

For example, when Abraham Lincoln prepared his Gettysburg Address (http://www.civilwar.org/education/history/primarysources), why did he begin with "Four score and seven years ago" rather than just giving a number? How does the parallel construction "of the people, by the people, and for the people" change how we read it? How does it affect what we feel about this moment in history? About this nation? About ourselves and our relationship to our nation's government? What is Lincoln's purpose here? In discussing Lincoln's address, the reader may well ask, From what does that meaning derive, aside from words and their arrangement? This approach invites students to analyze the many choices the writer has made in crafting the text as well as what other choices *could* have been made.

SELECTING MODELS FOR READING

The reading of texts that will offer models with high standards for our student writers is clearly a useful strategy, and several recent books and articles are helpful in locating books and passages we can use to inspire our students. Ruth Culham (2014) and Stephanie Harvey and Anne Goudvis (2007) are particularly good at providing ideas for using reading to inspire our young writers. If we seek to develop our skills as teachers and our students' skills as readers and writers, we will search our horizons for texts that inform, edify, clarify, and inspire.

A good reader notices and considers skillful word choice, powerful sentence structure, or a brilliantly written paragraph. That is what we should ask of all our students. In fact, we can teach students fairly early in their years in school to evaluate what they read, and the more skillful the writer, the more we hope they will admire!

A worthy writing model is essential to writers and can take diverse forms, including an essay, a newspaper or magazine article, an intriguing passage from a novel, a short scene from a play, or even a comic strip. The objective is to investigate how elements chosen by the author contribute to meaning. Why this word and not a different word? This is called diction, or word choice. Why is this detail included? A good writer is deliberate. Is there metaphorical language or sensory appeal? This is called imagery.

A more difficult challenge is recognizing syntax as key to communication. Why a short sentence? Why a long sentence? How does a complex sentence lend itself to this particular idea's best expression? Practice of this kind makes sleuths out of readers. Yet even a first grader can point out a word she likes, and a teacher can help her articulate why she likes it. Teachers are coaching students to notice what is on the page and then allowing them time for the text itself to reveal to them the significance of that choice in establishing meaning. What do students see? What is the impact of what they notice on their construction of meaning? In getting closer to the actual text, students practice putting themselves in the position of the writer, choosing and arranging words, one at a time. (See Activity 1.1: *Take Time to Notice—Looking and Learning*.) Let's talk together about how writers make meaning with their words.

An acronym that can help guide students to recognize an author's purpose through noticing the writer's choices is DIDLS, the letters of which represent the major elements that contribute to the determination of *form* and *tone*:

> *D* is for *Diction* (also called word choice)
> *I* is for *Imagery*
> *D* is for *Detail*
> *L* is for *Language* (formal? educated? religious? military?)
> *S* is for *Syntax* (also called sentence structure)

(See Activities 1.4, 1.5, and 1.6: *Noticing the Writer's Choices*. These activities offer guidance in using DIDLS to teach close reading in both poetry and prose.)

Learning to compare and contrast two written works (Common Core Anchor Reading Standard 9) can be difficult to achieve. Readers do it without even noticing when they express their preferences. When a student says, "I didn't like that assigned reading," the teacher has the opportunity to ask, What didn't you like? What could the author have done differently? Teachers, when working with younger children or with reluctant readers and writers, are not looking for a "right answer" as much as an honest reader response. The value of the question is in the challenge it provides for students to explain *why* it appeals to them.

It is most important that students articulate the reasons for their response based on textual evidence (Common Core Anchor Writing Standard 9). Teachers often imagine that comprehension is the gold standard and that application or analysis is somewhere beyond that. The responses that teachers get from students may not reach a high level right away, but teachers/coaches can encourage them, as they grow, to notice the word, the detail, or the sentence construction; to reread when full understanding takes a little longer; and to ask higher-level questions.

DENOTATION AND CONNOTATION

It is important that students recognize the difference between the denotation and connotation of words. *Denotation* is simply the definition of a word, the usual way we ask students to define a term. This is too shallow for higher-level literacy. We also need to determine a word's emotional content, its "baggage." When students write, they need to consider their intent and choose their words accordingly.

English is so rich; we speakers of English often have dozens of words to choose from such that we can tailor our message to deliver a broad spectrum of emotions. Only by reading and discerning the writers' choices can educators help students weigh their own words when they write. That emotional baggage is the *connotation* of words. It involves the heart as well as the brain. It tells us how we feel about what we read. (See Activity 1.7: *Determining Connotation vs. Denotation—Taking the Temperature of Words*, which offers practice in identifying the degree of emotion attached to a word.)

IT HELPS TO ASK THE RIGHT QUESTION!

We have an important tool for raising our students' level of critical thinking, and that is teaching students to recognize the value of the right question. Inquiry is a catalyst not only to better thinking but also to motivation. With their students, teachers can distinguish the level and purpose of the question by using Bloom's (1976) Taxonomy. Teachers will write prompts and discussion questions or focus questions. Rather than relegate this most useful tool to the training of future educators, the levels of questioning can easily be used in a secondary classroom to support and inspire students to frame the best question, which is often as powerful as the "right" answer. Students can write their own questions about their reading for Literature Circles (Daniels, 2002) or for small-group discussion. Teach students how important it is to frame a question by modeling the application of Bloom's Taxonomy in the classroom.

For the purposes of this book, we will be using the language from the original Bloom's Taxonomy. However, a simpler structure for questioning based on levels is written below and can also be effective. Put "three levels of questions" in the search box at the website http://www.wsfcs.k12.nc.us:

- *Level 1*—questions can be answered explicitly by facts contained in the text or by information accessible in other resources.
- *Level 2*—questions are textually implicit, requiring analysis and interpretation of specific parts of the text.

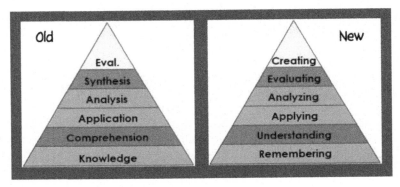

Bloom's Taxonomy
Creative Commons

- *Level 3*—questions are much more open ended and go beyond the text. They are intended to provoke a discussion of an abstract idea or issue or to make connections with other texts. This level includes what we call "Essential Questions."

Students can write their own questions and work together to separate them into the three categories, depending on the purpose of the question. Teachers will foster higher-level thinking by framing questions wisely.

The more practice teachers give students in formulating their own questions, the better. Most people would agree that life has more questions than it has answers. Whenever students think in terms of questions rather than answers, they access a pathway to higher thinking. In all classes, we want to encourage questioning of events, actions, processes, results, applications, and decisions. (See Activity 1.8: *Identifying Three Kinds of Questions*.)

RESEARCH PAPERS IN ENGLISH CLASS

Teachers in content area subjects often expect English teachers to "teach the research paper" when in fact language arts as a subject has little need for research apart from perusal of literary criticism usually found at a postsecondary level. Research in English class often results in a simple report that lacks the meaningful "inquiry" that drives true research. That makes the research paper a good interdisciplinary project (Casey, 2013). There is, however, an alternative way to introduce students to research, and that is through the assigning of an I-Search paper (Assaf, Ash, Saunders, & Johnson, 2011).

In 1970, Ken Macrorie introduced the concept of the I-Search paper to encourage students to develop voice in a way that maintains the individuality and the integrity of the inquirer, who writes to explain and to celebrate findings. Later, in additional books, Macrorie (1988) developed and refined the idea of the I-Search. The process of investigation is documented, from simply wondering about something to following ideas through to conclusions after curiosity has been fully satisfied.

A student might have questions about a career, such as justice or nursing—what does a student want to know? Their wanting to know about the topic fuels the search. They could explore a concept, searching for answers in poetry and not stopping with a dictionary definition. What might happen if we were to examine a topic like friendship? Or liberty? Or war? Approaching the research paper from an I-Search perspective develops the executive power of the writer as he or she probes the subject of interest. This is a project well suited to a language arts classroom. (See Activity 1.9: *Using the I-Search Paper.*)

Notice how these skills transfer seamlessly from English language arts into content area literacy. If one can help students identify in their reading the attitude and choices of the author, students can better discern the author's purpose. The ability to be a discerning reader is as essential to any content area as it is to English. These skills are crucial anywhere in the curriculum where an author puts forth an opinion or a point of view. The Common Core Standards (n.d.) recognize the responsibility of all teachers for their students' literacy skills. As stated in Anchor Writing Standard 7, "Conduct short as well as more sustained research projects based on focused questions, demonstrating understanding of the subject under investigation." Students' success with these new standards rests on *their* raising their critical skills through competent reading and writing.

Olson (2011), in *The Reading/Writing Connection*, notes that reading and writing have been seen in the past as "opposites," one passive and the other generative. She reinforces her contention that they are "similar processes of meaning construction" (p. 16), citing recent research. The National Institute of Child Health and Development Reading Writing Report reviews the present research on the reading writing connection and makes recommendations for more research to be done in the future.

GENERATING ACTIVITIES AND STRATEGIES THAT MOTIVATE AND EMPOWER

How can teachers motivate students to *help themselves* to develop these critical skills? Teachers can provide choices for students in their reading and writing topics. They can ensure that their reading and writing activities are authentic real-life activities that students clearly recognize as beneficial to them in their future lives. They can provide collaborative learning environments for literacy activities, providing numerous opportunities for student discourse. They can provide proper scaffolding in reading and writing activities to ensure that students are learning in their "zone of proximal development" (Vygotsky, 1997) and at their own instructional level. Additionally, they can provide clear feedback to students regarding their reading and writing products—both formatively and summatively. Most important, students must be motivated and actively engaged in the reading/writing process.

Teachers can make it fun to celebrate great words and to notice interesting details as the class reads. Students can read short, engaging works to practice skills. Teachers can be ever on the lookout for good writing and can express why they think it is good. Guthrie and Wigfield (2000) say it best: It is likely that motivational processes are the foundation for coordinating cognitive goals and strategies in reading. National, state, or local standards will set the bar.

ACTIVITIES FOR CHAPTER 1

These activities address the Common Core Standards for reading and writing, providing teachers with a shared vision of literacy across the disciplines. The following standards in both reading and writing govern the suggested strategies that follow.

Target Anchor Standards for Reading

Standard 1. Read closely to determine what the text says explicitly and to make logical inferences from it; cite specific textual evidence when writing or speaking to support conclusions drawn from the text.
Standard 4. Interpret words and phrases as they are used in the text, determining technical, connotative, and figurative meanings, and analyze how specific word choices shape meaning or tone.
Standard 5. Analyze the structure of texts, including how specific sentences, paragraphs, and larger portions of the text . . . relate to each other and the whole.

Target Anchor Standards for Writing

Standard 4. Produce clear and coherent writing in which the development, organization, and style are appropriate to task, purpose, and audience.
Standard 9. Draw evidence from literary or informational texts to support analysis, reflection, and research.

Activity 1.1: *Take Time to Notice—Looking and Learning*

Learner Objective

Students will observe and respond to what they see. This activity promotes discernment and may be used across the content areas. Noticing is the first step toward improved discernment that is transferable to reading and writing. This prewriting activity helps students attain a higher level of thinking. Everyone can begin by noticing *something* (Barry, 2012).

Assignment

Begin class by spending some time looking at a picture, an illustration, or a cartoon. What do you notice? Where is your eye drawn first? Why? What does the arrangement of objects have to say about them and about you, the viewer? Even preschoolers can be taught to patiently observe and respond to a picture. Take time out of a high school or middle school day to practice observation skills.

Everything learned from viewing pictures is applicable to observing text. Just as we can learn the terms of art for discussing a picture, we can learn the vocabulary that will facilitate conversations about reading and writing (Fenton & Charron, 2016). We can move more quickly beyond the superficial conversation about what happened, who it happened to, and so on to the deeper questions concerning *how* and *why*. Go to a page of text in any content area and let it speak. Notice the author's deliberate selection of words and their arrangement, the elements of form, and the nuance of tone. It may sound like a difficult or complicated skill, but it is actually very easy to help students to achieve a higher level of thinking (Self, 2013).

Teacher Resources

1. The Smithsonian American Art Museum and the Renwick Gallery offer a plethora of visual images that may be used for observational purposes. Visual images range from paintings, photographs, and sculptures from all eras to student podcasts where students demonstrate their observational and critical thinking skills. http://americanart.si.edu/education/resources/activities
2. The National Art Education Association website has visual images that may also be used for observation purposes. http://www.arteducators.org/learning
3. https://student.societyforscience.org provides relevant science visuals for students.

Formative Assessment

Teacher anecdotal records may be used to guide future activities. Have a notebook with a tab for each student. As you walk around during small-group discussions, make note of individual students' personal interests, strengths, and weaknesses to use in future activities. Note which students require more support. These observations provide valid data to use for parent–teacher conferences and report card comments.

Universal Design for Learning Application

Engagement (stimulate interest and motivation for learning)—Allow students to choose an image or a passage from an area of their own personal interest.

Students Who Require Extensive Support

Expand students' language through the use of "vocabulary pages" in a section in a language arts notebook. Students may develop word lists of sensory terms, verbs, adjectives, and so on: *see, notice, observe, perceive, spot, witness, distinguish, discern, detect.* This particularly assists students who think literally and require explicit instruction in expanding and understanding vocabulary. Students benefit from developing vocabulary portfolios they can refer to whenever they write. Vocabulary pages may be laminated and placed in a notebook for students to refer to while writing or kept in an electronic portfolio on the computer. This benefits literal thinkers, students with memory deficits, and students who require overlearning of concepts and procedures (Rohrer, Taylor, Pashler, Wixted, & Cepeda, 2005). Clip art pictures may be added to ensure understanding.

see, notice, observe, perceive, spot . . .

I _____ *the bird.*

Provide a choice of "images or passages" for those students who require more guidance.

Representation (present information and content in different ways)—Images or passages may be presented to students in a variety of formats: a page in a book, a passage viewed online, an image from a website page, a painting or sculpture in a museum, an artifact brought in by the teacher, a video, an audio recording. Have the students offer input on how they would like their image or passage presented to them.

Action and expression (differentiate the ways that students can express what they know)—Allow students to work in small groups to facilitate discussion of their observations and to give them an understanding of differences in the way individuals view ideas, passages, and images. This is a wonderful way to introduce "perspective" to students. Students may want to show their perspectives visually through their own images or diagrams. Students may benefit from taking their own photographs to use in their small-group discussions.

Activity 1.2: *Take Time to Notice—An Artist's Choices*

Learner Objective

Students describe similarities and differences in various works of art. This activity uses art to develop skill in noticing.

Assignment

With the class, discover ways in which works of art and written language are alike and how they are different in the ways they evoke emotion. If the class has been introduced to the tone acronym DIDLS (see the section "Selecting Models for Reading" in this chapter), develop a parallel list of elements from writing and from art, both representing choices the artist has made. Both art and writing are called "compositions." Why? Students should discover that both have a subject that is communicated to an audience, and both are creative works of an "artist." Paintings have shades of light and dark. They have color and line and shape. How are these communicated in prose or poetry? Which elements reveal the "tone" of a painting? How are imagery and detail incorporated in the medium? Develop a vocabulary list for describing both media.

Apply vocabulary to the question of how artists convey emotion by asking a social studies (or English) class to view a work of art that has a clear historical context, such as Pablo Picasso's painting *Guernica*. See Wikipedia or another site to find an image of the work for the class to view so that you can observe and discuss it together. *Guernica* is a painting about the chaos and suffering associated with the Spanish Civil War. Ask students the following:

- Where does your eye go first? Why?
- What do you notice? Create a list of 10 things you notice.
- What emotions are conveyed through these elements?
- What would you conclude is the message of this work of art?

Then have students (or several students) research the history of Spain and the creation of *Guernica*. If there is time, view some other paintings by Picasso. How does the response of the viewer to this work compare to the response to a realistic depiction of war? How does an artist or writer interpret the history and culture in which he or she lives?

Compare the response of today's students to the response of students in Picasso's time to the painting *Guernica*. Then read and discuss a war poem, such as Wilfred Owen's "Dulce et Decorum Est." See http://www.warpoetry.co.uk for more poems on this subject. This is a project that naturally combines social studies and English and would invite a cross-disciplinary collaboration.

Any image of interest in any content area that conveys emotion is worth our analysis. One example is *The Migrant Mother* photograph taken in the 1930s by Dorothea Lange. (Google the image of *The Migrant Mother*.) Let the photo launch critical and creative discussion into the value of cross-disciplinary study. Use it as a catalyst both for historical reading and for historical novels, such as Karen Hess's young adult novel *Out of the Dust* or John Steinbeck's *Grapes of Wrath*.

Formative Assessment

Teacher anecdotal records may be used to guide future activities. Have a notebook with a tab for each student. As you walk around during small-group discussions, make note of individual students' personal interests, strengths, and weaknesses to use in future activities. Note which students require more support in developing their background knowledge of the topic. Set up a small-group session to provide these students the time and means to increase their background understanding. This background knowledge will support future understandings about the topic.

Universal Design for Learning Application

  Engagement (stimulate interest and motivation for learning)—Allow students to choose a topic they are interested in. Provide a list of "topics" for those students who require more guidance.

  Representation (present information and content in different ways)—Present information using a variety of different options: websites, author talks, Ted talks, YouTube videos etc.

  Action and expression (differentiate the ways that students can express what they know)—Allow students to demonstrate their understanding by giving them a variety of choices: small-group verbal presentation, poster presentation, video presentation, role play, and so on.

Activity 1.3: *Take Time to Notice—Comparison of Two Works of Art*

Learner Objective

Students extend their comparative observations using two works of art.

Assignment

Have students first view Henri Matisse's painting *Woman in a Purple Coat* by accessing the website of the Museum of Fine Arts, Houston.

Ask students what they notice, using the terms of art developed in Activity 1.1. Follow up with the following questions:

- Where did your eye go first?
- What can you tell about this woman from the painting?
- What might be the occasion of the painting?
- What is the effect of the busy patterns? Of the colors?
- Do you think she picked and arranged the flowers?
- Do you think she plans to eat the fruit?

Woman in a Purple Coat by Henri Matisse
Museum of Fine Arts, Houston

Then have students view Primrose McPherson Paschal's painting titled *Beulah's Baby*, found on North Carolina Museum of Art website.

- Where did your eye go first? Why?
- How is it similar to Matisse's work? How is it different?
- What can you tell about her life?
- How is the emotion in this painting communicated?

Beulah's Baby, 1948 by Primrose McPherson Paschal
North Carolina Museum of Art, Raleigh

- What do the colors suggest? Look at Renaissance paintings of the Madonna and draw some conclusions.

If possible, end by looking at the two paintings side by side to accentuate the comparison. Discuss the cultural differences that resulted in the comparison. This lesson might also lead to a comparison of two poems with similar themes but different attitudes, like Edgar Allen Poe's "To Helen" and Hilda Dolittle's poem "Helen." Examine similar themes and different cultures but also examine different viewpoints and the same culture.

In either social studies or English class, ask students to compare the messages conveyed in Picasso's *Guernica* and in earlier artist Francisco Goya's *Mars Devouring*

His Son, also translated *Mars Eating His Children*. Who is "Mars"? How might he be eating "his children"?

How does "close reading" of art or "close reading" of written works help us interpret the meaning through *noticing* the choices that an artist/writer has deliberately made?

Teacher Resources

1. The Smithsonian American Art Museum and the Renwick Gallery offer a plethora of visual images that may be used for observational purposes. Visual images range from paintings, photographs, and sculptures from all eras to student podcasts where students demonstrate their observational and critical thinking skills. http://americanart.si.edu/education/resources/activities
2. The National Art Education Association website also has visual images that may be used for observation purposes. http://www.arteducators.org/learning
3. https://student.societyforscience.org provides relevant science visuals for students.

Formative Assessment

Teachers will identify which students are ready to move on to Activity 1.4 by observing their verbal responses to the assignments in Activities 1.1 to 1.3. Teachers identify students' understanding of the terms *diction, imagery, detail, language,* and *syntax*. Once students can identify these features in text, they are ready to incorporate these features into their writing. Teachers may want to introduce one feature at a time for students to include in their writing, eventually having students attempt to identify and thoughtfully consider each of the DIDLS features in their writing. A simple rubric can assist teachers in keeping track of students' understandings, allowing teachers to form small student groups for reteaching and reinforcement of previous DIDLS components.

Class _____ *Date* _____

✔ +   **✔**   **✔ -**

Exemplary   *Proficient*   *Needs Improvement*

Student Names	Content Area Understanding	D Diction	I Imagery	D Detail	L Language	S Syntax

Universal Design for Learning Application

> *Engagement (stimulate interest and motivation for learning)*—Allow students to choose an object/picture of their choice representing their personal interests.
>
> *Representation (present information and content in different ways)*—Object or picture may be in paper format, photograph taken at a museum or any other site, personal painting, or something viewed online.
>
> *Action and expression (differentiate the ways that students can express what they know)*—Allow students to demonstrate their understanding through writing by producing PowerPoints or Prezis or producing a project-based demonstration of knowledge, possibly a visual poster representation of their understanding.

Activity 1.4: *Noticing the Writer's Choices — Reading Poems*

Learner Objective

Students describe how writers' choices impact meaning. This activity extends the "noticing" in Activity 1.1 to choices made in various written texts.

Assignment

An acronym that helps guide students to recognize the author's purpose through noticing the writer's choices is DIDLS, which identifies the major elements of *form* and *tone*. These exercises will help students develop their powers of observation in *any text*:

> *D* is for *Diction*, which means word choice. Why that word and not another?
> *I* is for *Imagery* and includes all figurative or sensory choices.
> *D* is for *Detail*. Good writers have a reason for inclusion of a detail.
> *L* is for *Language* (formal? educated? religious? military?). How can we characterize?
> *S* is for *Syntax*, or sentence structure. This is also the writer's choice.

Apply DIDLS to a favorite poem, perhaps "The Road Not Taken" by Robert Frost. What do you notice? Which elements best point the way to meaning? What is the poem *really* about? Find examples of effective diction (the word *diverged*), important images (a road divided in two), telling details (the woods were *yellow*), and sentences that are constructed by the poet for a certain effect. (What about the construction of that first sentence? Why so long and complex? How does the sentence mirror what he is doing?) Check for understanding of syntax and Frost's lack of punctuation in lines 2 to 5 in the first stanza. How should we read it aloud to promote the reader's understanding of that sentence? Notice repeating words and how they add structure to the poem. Let students mark up what they notice, then do it together on a "smart board," if available. An interesting question: Frost chooses to finish the poem by rhyming *hence* and *difference*, which look the same but are imperfect rhymes. What might be the effect of this "near" or "visual" rhyme on the reader? Finally, consider opening the discussion to consider rhythm (meter) and rhyme if you wish to widen the lesson to more general consideration of a poet's choices. See chapter 5 for further discussion of poetry and writing.

Students Who Require Extensive Support

Students who require extensive support need many examples in order to understand figurative language. Keeping these examples in a language arts notebook allows students to refer back to these concepts as needed. For example, write the definition of a metaphor and then provide the students "captioned" pictures with a sentence under the picture using the metaphor. Expand the notebook as figurative language is introduced to include captioned visual examples of similes, personification, hyperboles, and so on. Clip art pictures may be added to ensure understanding.

Formative Assessment

Use a chart to track students' understanding of DIDLS, from diction and detail to imagery and finally on to language and syntax. This chart will guide future whole-group and small-group instruction.

Universal Design for Learning Application

Engagement (stimulate interest and motivation for learning)—Have students choose poetry appropriate to their level and interest. Pair students to facilitate sharing and understanding.

Representation (present information and content in different ways)—Students may use poetry from books, websites, YouTube, or teacher-provided poetry. If necessary, use a program where text may be highlighted and then read out loud to the student. A graphic organizer showing DIDLS will assist students in identifying what they have noticed. For poetry, encourage students to also notice rhyme, rhythm, and repetition.

Action and expression (differentiate the ways that students can express what they know)—Have students work in pairs to share what they noticed. Allow students to share their understandings in any format that makes sense to them: Power-Points, Prezis, posters, illustrations, diagrams, and so on.

Activity 1.5: *Noticing the Writer's Choices—Reading Fiction*

Learner Objective

Students will notice the choices a writer makes when constructing a narrative.

Assignment

This activity models a close reading process applying DIDLS as a close reading aid. The protocol can be adapted to any level, using a text that is appropriate to students. Younger students can begin by concentrating on diction and detail, then adding imagery. Do not, however, conclude that language and syntax are beyond their level. Most students looking at this passage from Charles Dickens's *Great Expectations* would tell you that Magwich lacks education. Most students can compare longer and shorter sentences and offer reasons for a writer's choices.

For this specific assignment, provide students with a copy of the first page of chapter 42 of *Great Expectations*. Ask students to identify DIDLS by rereading and marking what they notice. Then have them use "the evidence" they found to answer the questions and guide their thinking.

The context: The convict Magwich is, in fact, Pip's actual benefactor, not Miss Havisham, as Pip assumed. In this passage, Magwich addresses Pip and Herbert Pocket, Pip's roommate and friend. (To locate this passage in the text, see chapter 42 of *Great Expectations*, from the beginning of the chapter):

> Dear boy and Pip's comrade, I am not a-going fur to tell you my life, like a song or a story-book. But to give it you short and handy, I'll put it at once into a mouthful of English. In jail and out of jail, in jail and out of jail, in jail and out of jail. There, you've got it. That's my life pretty much, down to such times as I got shipped off, arter Pip stood my friend.
>
> I've been done everything to, pretty well—except hanged. I've been locked up, as much as a silver tea-kettle. I've been carted here and carted there, and put out of this town and put out of that town, and stuck in the stocks, and whipped and worried and drove. I've no more notion where I was born than you have—if so much. I first become aware of myself, down in Essex, a-thieving turnips for my living. Summun had run away from me—a man—a tinker—and he'd took the fire with him, and left me wery cold.
>
> I know'd my name to be Magwich, chrisen'd Abel. How did I know it? Much as I know'd the birds' names in the hedges to be chaffinch, sparer, thrush. I might have thought it was all lies together, only as the birds' names come out true, I supposed mine did.
>
> So fur as I could find, there warn't a soul that see young Abel Magwich, with as little on him as in him, but wot caught fright at him, and either drove him off, or took him up. I was took up, took up, took up, to that extent I reg'larly grow'd up took up.

After students have marked this text for what they might have noticed, have them determine which elements are key to understanding Magwich's message. Have them choose which two or three elements (DIDLS) are key to understanding the passage and the meaning it contributes to the reading of this novel. The following discussion questions are models provided by the authors to structure the DIDLS application. Questions are meant as spurs to the final discovery of meaning:

Concerning *diction*:

- To whom is this speech addressed?
- What attitude is conveyed in Magwich's choice of terms?
- What do his word choices tell us about Magwich as a human being?
- Which words stand out and carry the weight of his meaning as he wished to be understood?

Concerning *imagery*:

- Which words can we associate with Magwich? What emotions/feelings "rub off"?
- How do opposites work here? Which align with meaning? Which show the opposite to suggest what is true?
- What connotations can we attribute to his using the names of birds?
- How does a silver tea-kettle alter the reader's thinking about Magwich?

Concerning *detail*:

- Make a list of objects and their details
- Explain what each adds by simply *being* there. How does their inclusion affect a reader's expectations?
- Are these all factual details? How do these details influence the *affect*, or emotional value, of the passage?

Concerning *language*: Magwich's language is important! A reader needs to get "down and dirty" about what his language really tells us about him—and the society Pip considers himself to be part of. Note that Magwich's socioeconomic status has power to change the reader's assessment of him. Then as now, socioeconomic status has influence on people and people's thinking:

- Catalog his speech peculiarities. What does speech reveal about a society and the people in it?
- What does it tell us about this time and place?
- How do the contradictions on this page help bring the situation to its ultimate resolution?

Concerning *syntax*:

- How are Magwich's thoughts constructed?
- Is this an argument? Analyze its logic.

- How does its syntax affect (or reflect) the logic of the piece?
- Find a short sentence and a longer sentence. How does each accomplish its purpose?

The *big question*, after consideration of all we have discovered in examining DIDLS, is, How does the form of this passage contribute to its meaning?

Formative Assessment: After students discuss their "markups," the teacher may collect their papers to ensure understanding. Students may now begin to deliberately use and discuss DIDLS in their own writing.

Universal Design for Learning Application

Engagement (stimulate interest and motivation for learning)—Have students choose text appropriate to their level and interest. Pair students to facilitate sharing and understanding.

Representation (present information and content in different ways)—Students may use fiction text from books. If necessary, use a program where text may be highlighted and then read out loud to the student. A graphic organizer showing DIDLS will assist students in identifying what they have noticed.

Action and expression (differentiate the ways that students can express what they know)—Have students work in pairs to share what they noticed. Students may share by talking or by creating a visual representation of their learning.

Activity 1.6: *Noticing the Writer's Choices—Reading Nonfiction*

Learner Objective

The student will ascertain the choices and attitudes of the writer.

Assignment

Assign a short passage from class reading that seems significant for any reason, perhaps a passage from a good newspaper article, a passage from a famous speech, or a passage from the writings of Nelson Mandela, John Muir, or Alexis de Tocqueville. Try the autobiography of Benjamin Franklin—or a speech given by Susan B. Anthony. Anything that is nonfiction will work. Ask students to choose a passage, a paragraph, or a page from class reading that they think has some importance. Identify *which elements* (DIDLS) seem to contribute the most to constructing meaning. Higher-level students can critique the choices made by the author once they determine the purpose of the piece. Can the attitude of the writer be determined from the choices the writer made? (Chapter 3 on essay writing will further analyze writing that is persuasive.)

Have students choose one element of DIDLS and demonstrate how they can see the attitude of the writer in the text.

Universal Design for Learning Application

Engagement (stimulate interest and motivation for learning)—Allow students to choose the work they would like to read from a list provided by the teacher that ensures content rigor and access.

Representation (present information and content in different ways)—Apply DIDLS to a variety of genres. Find editorials or a relevant cartoon in the area of social studies, mathematics, or science to put on students' "choose from" list.

Action and expression (differentiate the ways that students can express what they know)—Allow students to demonstrate their understanding through writing by producing PowerPoints or Prezis, writing out and role-playing simulations, or producing a project-based demonstration of knowledge—possibly a visual poster representation of their understanding.

Activity 1.7: Determining Connotation vs. Denotation—Taking the Temperature of Words

Learner Objective

Students will distinguish between connotation and denotation, between the emotion and the literal meaning conveyed by words. This activity teaches students that words have an emotional value in addition to a dictionary meaning. Students will more carefully evaluate word choice in reading and writing.

Assignment

Make sure that students know the meaning of the words *connotation*, *denotation*, and *effect* (n.) versus *affect* (n.) (key off the word *affection*, which they will understand). Have students brainstorm all the words they can think of for the word *underweight*. When they run out of synonyms, collect their word bank onto the whiteboard. The list will include such words as *skinny, slim, thin, scrawny, slender, emaciated*, and so on. Once you have collected as many synonyms as the class can think of, ask students to put a plus sign (+) next to all those they might use to describe someone they care about—perhaps a friend or sibling. Then they should put a minus sign (–) next to those they would reserve for someone they thought less of or were angry with—perhaps an enemy.

Have students arrange the words around the neutral word *underweight*, putting them in order from the most negative to the most positive. Words carry emotional

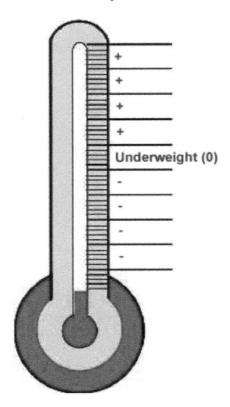

Students Who Require Extensive Support

Traditional graphic organizers may be modified to encourage understanding for those students who require a more linear visual approach for understanding vocabulary. Using visuals in conjunction with authentic experiences and artifacts facilitates learning for a wide array of learners, including but not limited to autism spectrum disorders, intellectual disabilities, English Language Learners, and deaf students. For instance, write the following words in a linear fashion providing a picture (clip art or photograph) under each word to ensure understanding of the meaning of the word. Add these pages to the students' language arts notebooks for future reference. The following graphic organizer may be modified by simply adding a visual to go along with the written word. Clip art pictures may be added under each word to ensure understanding.

"baggage" that should be recognized by a reader or a writer. Notice affect and how it can make a message more interesting—and more powerful!

Formative Assessment

This is a warm-up activity for writing. Through observation of student responses, teachers determine students' understanding of the emotional content of words.

Universal Design for Learning Application

Engagement (stimulate interest and motivation for learning)—Allow students to choose the words they would like to use for their "thermometer." Provide a choice of word lists for those students who require more guidance.

Representation (present information and content in different ways)—Present information using the "thermometer model" and the "linear visual picture model" when modeling information to the class.

Action and expression (differentiate the ways that students can express what they know)—Allow students to demonstrate their understanding through either the "thermometer model" or the "linear visual picture model." Students may want to use clip art from their computers for illustrations, or they may want to draw their own illustrations. Allow students to work in small groups to facilitate discussion of word choices, furthering concept understanding.

Activity 1.8: *Identifying Three Kinds of Questions*

Learner Objectives

Students will formulate questions for various purposes. This activity helps students delve into text and raises awareness of the different types of questions that can be applied to students' reading or writing. This spells out to students that not only teachers ask questions. It is the job of students to formulate questions as well. This raises students' critical thinking skills as they maneuver through the different levels of questions. Critical thinking skills positively impact both reading and writing. The same types of questions could be asked of students' own writing. Students also will begin to understand how each question type serves a different purpose.

Assignment

Using any text that the class is currently talking about, write two questions that would suit each of the three purposes listed below. Some examples follow:

- *Focus questions*: In *The Hunger Games* (Collins, 2008): Who is Prim? (level 1). Why did Katniss, the protagonist, volunteer to fill her sister Prim's place? (level 2).

- *Open-ended questions*: The best questions for discussion go beyond "what?" and "who?" to "why?" and "how?" Compare Peeta and Gale. Argue *why* Katniss should choose one rather than the other. (This question is level 3, an open-ended question that should result in good discussion.) If you were a contender, would you join up to kill an opponent? *Evaluate* Katniss's decisions. What decisions would you make? Why? (level 3).

Students Who Require Extensive Support

Having students work in collaborative groups to develop questions scaffolds student learning. Conversations should be supplemented with a visual form of the questions as they evolve. In addressing the essential questions, some students may require skill-based small-group instruction that preteaches essential question concepts through examples with visuals to support understanding.

What effect can a government or society have on individual behavior?

Make a visual time line of the above question by inserting pictures under the sentence below.

Government   makes laws   that affect   individual behavior.

Clip art may be inserted under words to ensure understanding.

Students Who Require Extensive Support

Students may need guided assistance when answering questions based on Bloom's Taxonomy. Teachers need to provide much practice on answering each level of question. When possible, provide students written forms of the question along with the oral form of the question. If questions are currently too difficult for a particular student, adapt the question by moving down the Bloom's Taxonomy scale until the student is successful. Mix up questions for your Socratic seminars (see chapter 2) and have the student who needs extensive support answer the lower-level questions while others answer the open-ended questions. Even students who require extensive support can often do the same activities as the general education students. Using the above ideas along with simplified adapted visuals and shortened assignments makes the above content area activity accessible to all. Students may not be able to rewrite a historical document, but they can certainly write a caption, paragraph, or page on a historical picture.

- *Essential questions*: What effect can a government or society have on individual behavior? Are human beings always responsible for their own actions? What can an individual do to change a decadent, corrupt, or immoral society? (level 3).

For the purposes of this book, we will be using the headings from the original Bloom's Taxonomy (http://screencasting3point0.wikispaces.com/Bloom%27s+Taxonomy). For a simpler version of the levels for questions, see the section "It Helps to Ask the Right Question!" earlier in this chapter.

Formative Assessment

Teachers identify the level of questions that students draw from using Bloom's Taxonomy.

Universal Design for Learning Application

Engagement (stimulate interest and motivation for learning)—Allow students to choose a topic they are interested in when developing questions. For a specific content area, provide a choice of topics for students to choose from.

Representation (present information and content in different ways)—Introduce concepts using visuals to support understanding.

Action and expression (differentiate the ways that students can express what they know)—Allow students to demonstrate their understanding through writing by producing PowerPoints or Prezis, comic strip formats, or role-play interviews or by generating a project-based demonstration of knowledge—possibly a visual poster representation of their understanding.

Activity 1.9: *Using the I-Search Paper*

Learner Objective

Students collect, organize, and write information from many sources to satisfy their curiosity. This activity allows students to pursue authentic research, which is inherently motivational. Reading and writing are equally represented in the I-Search paper. Through this activity, students may employ all of the skills previously practiced from this chapter's assignments.

Assignment

Using the I-Search paper in a variety of content areas creates an interdisciplinary approach and fulfills some of the stated Common Core Anchor Standards. Providing students with clear boundaries and a framework is a good approach. Offering a list of suggested topics gets the ideas churning, and students use that suggested list as a springboard for their own topics. Students can choose topics such as the following:

- Investigating a career
- A special interest or hobby, such as quilting
- A historical issue, such as the design for the 9/11 Memorial
- A particular holiday, such as Thanksgiving

Information for this type of research may be found in a variety of resources. It may include a poem, an oral history, an artifact, or an interview. For example, investigating a career could include interviewing nurses, or for the quilting choice, it may include a discussion of Alice Walker's (2003) short story "Everyday Use" (*Love and Trouble: Stories of Black Women*). For the 9/11 topic, perhaps taking a virtual or actual visit to the 9/11 site would be a good idea. A student might investigate family history involvement in the military and include a collection of photographs. If a student is doing a paper on the 1940s in America, he or she might interview a relative. Specific information on using the I-Search paper can be found at the following site:

http://www.readwritethink.org/professional-development/strategy-guides/promoting -student-directed-inquiry-30783.html.

Students Who Require Extensive Support

Tangibles can be used to teach punctuation to students who require extensive support. This aids the students' motivation as they consider the tangibles "fun" and also serves to focus students' attention on the task at hand. For instance, small stickers can be used as ending marks. Teachers can put ending marks on each sticker and have the student put the appropriate sticker at the end of the sentence. Stickers can also be used with uppercase letters on them to place on the first word of each sentence. Simple rubrics can be developed using the same concept. These would be used only with students who are many years below grade level.

Formative Assessment

Developing a topic of interest and finding source materials can be monitored by the teacher to determine if the student is ready to start reading.

Summative Assessment

The final product (research paper) indicates students' learnings and their ability to provide evidence and/or support for research ideas in writing.

Universal Design for Learning Application

Engagement (stimulate interest and motivation for learning)—Allow students to choose the topic they would like to use for their I-Search paper. Provide a choice of "topics" for those students who require more guidance.

Representation (present information and content in different ways)—Present information using videos, recordings, images, Ted talks, and so on. Personal interviews with individuals may also be used. Have the students develop the interview questions in order to facilitate engagement.

Action and expression (differentiate the ways that students can express what they know)—Allow students to demonstrate their understanding through Power-Points, Prezis, videos, or role plays or in a comic strip format. Students may want to use clip art from their computer for illustrations, or they may want to draw their own illustrations. Allow students to work in small groups to facilitate discussion of topics, furthering concept understanding.

2

Reading and Writing in the Content Areas

Clear writing is an essential ingredient of any communication and especially scientific communication. For example, in Science, we don't encourage clear writing, we insist on it.

—*Dr. Alan Leshner, chief executive officer,*
American Association for the Advancement of Science

All content area teachers should be literacy teachers who increase students' reading and writing skills while also increasing content area learning. The Carnegie Association of New York, in its publication *Reading Next: A Vision for Action and Research in Middle and High School Literacy* (Biancarosa & Snow, 2006), noted the importance of "effective instructional principles embedded in content using content-area texts" and also "content-area teachers providing instruction and practice."

There are numerous techniques to assist content area teachers in honing their instructional practices in the area of reading and writing (Guthrie & Klauda, 2014). How many social studies students are going to be historians? How many biology students will become biologists? Yet every student should be prepared to read and write about social studies and science in public media.

USING QUESTIONS TO TEACH IN THE CONTENT AREAS

In many content assignments, the use of Bloom's higher-level questions (see the section "It Helps to Ask the Right Question!" in chapter 1) encourages analysis and evaluation. When reading a prompt such as "In what ways was FDR's New Deal Program an untested idea?" students should employ higher-order key words, such as *interpret, evaluate, assess,* or *analyze* instead of *explain, list,* or *describe.*

In addition to providing focus or guiding questions to a lesson/unit of study on the Great Depression, content area teachers should challenge the students to read, think, and write in response to targeted essential questions, such as Was the Great Depression inevitable? Was the New Deal an effective response to the Depression? Did Franklin Roosevelt's New Deal weaken or save capitalism?

Content area teachers do not always succeed at engaging students in their learning. Teachers can, however, adopt some definite strategies that encourage engagement (Martinez, Yokota, & Temple, 2017; Wilhelm, 2007). Often, teachers use leading or focus questions, such as What have we just read? What is the piece telling us about our country? Why is this reading so important in our understanding of this time period? These are questions that will encourage learners to connect with the reading.

Some students may raise their hands, but others may be tuned out. Are teachers sufficiently engaging them in their learning or preparing them to be thinking citizens? Addressing questions orally, as well as in writing, teachers should use Bloom's Taxonomy to ensure higher-order thinking. Teachers may blame students for not studying, not caring, or not wanting to learn. Instead, teachers might ask, Why aren't students engaged in the learning? Why do they leave it to others to respond? Could writing make a difference? If every student has to write, at least there are better odds on some participation. Offering the students more opportunity for choice and creativity will engage them with their content reading and also address the Common Core Standards for Writing (Constable, Gross, Moniz, & Ryan, 2013).

WRITING WITH SOAPSTone

Ogden Morse (n.d.), consultant to the College Board, recommends SOAPSTone as a concrete strategy to help students identify and use certain central components as a basis for their own writing. SOAPSTone is an acronym especially useful for nonfiction and informational writing:

> *S* is for *Speaker*. Who is doing the writing or speaking?
> *O* is for *Occasion*. Presidential speech? Editorial? News article?
> *A* is for *Audience*. Who will read or hear this writing?
> *P* is for *Purpose*. What did the writer hope to accomplish?
> *S* is for *Subject*. What is the topic?
> *Tone*, which describes an author's attitude (ironic? flippant? angry?)

Once the SOAPSTone strategy has been taught, it can be used in a plethora of activities to enhance students' writing development in the content area. (See Activity 2.1: *Using the SOAPSTone Strategy*.)

ROLE PLAYING

Why role play? While increasing their literacy skills by writing dialogue, students, through role play, learn more about the time period of the event as well as about specific characters. Role play can be used across the disciplines. In social studies, students play roles of various characters in history or of people representative of an era. In science, students role-play scientific characters, such as Isaac Newton or Galileo (Monahan, 2013). In mathematics, students could role-play a mathematical genius, such as Albert Einstein and his ideas. Joan Schur (2007), an educational consultant in social studies and English and an author and adviser to schools, offers six multi-faceted eyewitness strategies in her approach to the teaching of history.

Schur (2007, p. vi) presents a way to instill life skills as well as historical and critical thinking skills in students. The written exercise can address the content reading not only on the time period and on a specific character but also on related vocabulary, sentence structure, tone, facts, and details. (See Activity 2.2: *Role Playing.*)

USING PRIMARY DOCUMENTS

Teachers can have students rewrite primary documents in student voice. This is a worthwhile exercise that stresses both reading and writing and finding the main ideas. Lesh (2011), a practicing high school teacher of history, offers a number of learning activities that could be used in rewriting a primary document. For students to think of history not as memorization but instead as the construction and evaluation of evidence-based arguments, they must do the following:

- See history as a discipline driven by questions.
- Understand the nature of historical evidence and be able to analyze a variety of sources and apply them to historical questions.
- Develop and defend evidence-based interpretations of the past (p. 4).

Doing the above in writing further develops students' reading and writing skills. The writing must be clear and based on evidence. Continually, connections must be made between reading and writing so that students use them in tandem.

In teaching the Rail Strike of 1877, Lesh (2011) provides a number of sources inclusive of but not limited to letters and flyers. In this literacy-rich activity, Lesh provides four documents that are discussed and placed in chronological order so that the students can then write the story of the strike, drawing from these documents along with other background information provided in books and online (p. 84). This activity could be used across the disciplines since it is asking students to dig deeper into knowledge through poignant, essential questions. (See Activity 2.3: *Using Primary Documents.*)

RESEARCH TO BUILD KNOWLEDGE: PROBLEM SOLVING

Providing a research question for students to find evidence (data) from multiple sources is key to students' developing their research skills. This is yet another opportunity for content area teachers to further students' reading and writing skills while increasing content area knowledge. Whether it is a scientific problem, a historical issue, or a current event, students can address the research in the form of a question to be investigated, researched, and presented in a variety of modalities, thus allowing access to the content area for all students. For example, why are volcanoes called active even when there is no eruption? Or how did Irish immigration impact Boston? This approach encourages critical thinking, assessment, and evaluation of content readings, leading to the development of the students' research skills.

USING ESSENTIAL QUESTIONS

To engage students in content area reading, teachers should use essential questions to encourage students to make connections between their reading and their prior knowledge (see chapter 1 for further explanation of essential questions). A question such as "Is war ever just?" or "What constitutes scientific proof?" can engage students much more quickly than listing the causes of the war or listing the results of a lab experiment. (See Activity 2.5: *Applying the Concept of Essential Questions in Content Areas*.)

IMPLEMENTING SOCRATIC SEMINARS

Seminars promote active learning in the content areas and offer teachers an opportunity to promote students' literacy skills. The Paideia Center, based on Mortimer Adler's work, has developed extensive materials on using seminars in classrooms and defines a Socratic seminar as a "collaborative, intellectual dialogue facilitated with open-ended questions about a text" (http://nwabr.org/sites/default/files/SocSem.pdf). You can review these principles online at http://www.paideia.org/about-paideia/philosophy.

The purpose of a Socratic seminar is to achieve a deeper understanding about the ideas and values in a text. In the seminar, participants systematically question and examine issues and principles related to a particular content area reading, and they articulate different points of view. The group conversation assists participants in constructing meaning through disciplined analysis, interpretation, listening, and participation.

In a Socratic seminar, the participants carry the burden of responsibility for the quality of the discussion. Good discussions occur when participants study the reading closely in advance, listen actively, share their ideas and questions in response to the ideas and questions of others, and search for evidence in the text to support their ideas. The discussion is not about right answers; it is not a debate. Students are encouraged to think out loud and to exchange ideas openly while examining ideas in a rigorous, thoughtful manner. Connecting the reading with discussion and follow-up writing just makes sense in using this seminar approach. *Read Write Think* offers suggestions for teachers who want to use this methodology (http://www.readwrite think.org/professional-development/strategy-guides/socratic-seminars-30600.html). (See Activity 2.6: *Implementing Socratic Seminars*.)

CRITICAL ANALYSIS OF TEXTBOOKS AND OTHER SOURCES OF INFORMATION

Rather than simply reading for information, students need to learn to critically analyze what they read and clearly express their thoughts in writing. Textbooks and other sources of information have points of view, audience, and tone in the presentation of the content. This provides an opportunity to compare textbooks with additional resources on a specific time period, such as the Gilded Age (late 19th century), or on a topic, such as the American labor movement.

Authors choose which details to include and in what order to present them. Are the points being made adequately supported? Are they compelling? Are they biased? Does the text present multiple viewpoints? Is this a text that I can learn from and with? What would I change in the text to make it better? This type of activity has students comparing various audiences and purposes, furthering text comprehension while honing writing skills (Charron, Fenton, Harris, & Procek, 2012). (See Activity 2.7: *Reviewing the Textbook*.)

In science, students can compare articles on the same topic from different sources: an article from *Scientific American*, an article from *Wired* or *Popular Science*, and a newspaper article. This type of activity has students comparing various audiences and purposes, furthering text comprehension while honing writing skills.

USING THE READER RESPONSE JOURNAL

The reader response journal is an excellent tool, but it must be seen as such by both students and teachers. The journal is an opportunity for students to practice different writing techniques. Journals may be used across the curriculum. Forcing students into journal writing will inspire love of neither reading nor writing. Teachers need to ask themselves, "What's in it for students? How can I use journal writing to engage students?"

Teachers should make it a habit to write and respond to student writing as fellow writers. It is important to leave an imprint on at least every third page so that students know the teacher has been there. The teacher, as a fellow reader/writer, should be drawn into discussion by a particularly thoughtful or interesting entry. To students, this is an intrinsic reward. Teachers should tell students that the more a reader feels compelled to reply, the more students know that the reader was impressed with their thinking. These are moments that teachers may share with the class if student writers concur. Many students will enjoy doing an interactive reading journal. Read Write Think's Literary Graffiti Interactive is a fun online journal tool (http://www.readwritethink.org/classroom-resources/lesson-plans/graffiti-wall-discussing-responding-208.html).

Teachers should grade journals on effort and thoughtfulness, not necessarily on brilliance, and definitely not on correctness. The journal should be rewarding to *everyone*. As a reader, the teacher should comment on the writer's thoughts, whatever they are, and allow students to respond honestly to their reading. Teachers can use the journal for formative assessment and for their own information. Making an appointment with students who need additional coaching and support scaffolds student writing and makes writing expectations clear. This is also a good time to offer suggestions for further readings.

Reader response journals can be used in any subject; however, coordinate their use with other subject teachers so that the students are not overloaded with journals. If the art teacher and the science teacher are also assigning journals, students will resent having to do one more. Journals should become a satisfying activity, not a chore. This is where interdisciplinary discussion with other teachers is essential. Why not motivate your students by doing online journaling? Penzu offers a secure free online journaling app for teachers and students to use (https://play.google.com/store/apps/details?id=com.penzu.android&hl=en or).

Some disciplines require more rigor and exactness in the journal than others. Correct information is essential in journals for some disciplines. The National Science Teachers Association offers information on science journals at http://www.nsta.org/publications/news/story.aspx?id=57384, and math journals may be investigated at http://interactive-math-science-notebooks.wikispaces.com.

Journal entries provide opportunity for students to expand their thinking into an essay or other longer, more purposeful forms. Regular practice requires that students read their past writing and evaluate its potential as a developed and finished product. (See Activity 2.8: *Journaling*.)

WRITING IN RESPONSE TO CONTENT PROMPTS

Much of content area writing at the middle school and high school levels involves students responding to prompts in their content area:

1. What factors significantly impacted our nation in the early 1900s? Include the Progressive movement, World War I, and the decade of the 1920s in your answer.

2. What processes occur during respiration?
3. Explain why the lowest carbon dioxide concentration occurs closest to the forest. Be sure to include a biological process in your answer.

Thus, this is a perfect opportunity for content area teachers to incorporate reading and writing instruction in conjunction with content area instruction. In order for content area readers to write coherently about what they read, they must learn to read nonfiction text with understanding (Goodwin & Miller, 2012/2013).

All learners often need a clear format to follow when reading nonfiction text. Having students fill out a graphic organizer before and during reading nonfiction text gives learners a visual guide to refer to when doing reader response activities. See the following website for text feature graphic organizers to use before and during reading: http://www.fcrr.org/FAIR_Search_Tool/FAIR_Search_Tool.aspx. (Click on Comprehension, Grade Level, and Expository Text.) This will greatly help students who have organizational, focusing, memory, communication, and language difficulties. Different graphic organizers serve different purposes. More information on this process may be found at http://www.readingrockets.org/article/52137. (See Activity 2.9: *Authentic Content Area Writing*.)

PRIOR READING OF NONFICTION TEXT

The Common Core Standards address the need for reading more nonfiction. A student studying any content area can find literature in the form of books, articles, excerpts, short stories, memoirs, and biographies that enlighten the reader and enhance the learning experience. Engaging students in writing about their reading encourages more participation and provides the teacher with vital formative assessments of student understanding of the content.

Training students in a process to use *before* reading the text prepares them to comprehend the nonfiction text that they read. Subsequently, it ensures that these students have the understanding to do their reader response activities. Initially, this approach may be a time-consuming activity, but once students develop proficiency in learning how to read nonfiction text, this process becomes less time consuming.

Some students may *always* need to use a graphic organizer before reading nonfiction text (http://www.readwritethink.org/classroom-resources/lesson-plans/using-thieves-preview-nonfiction-112.html). Others may be "weaned" from writing on the graphic organizer and may learn to follow these steps without writing down any of the information. The *Gradual Release of Responsibility Model* explains how teachers should progress from offering substantial support through *modeling a strategy* for the student to *jointly implementing the strategy* with the student to having the student *use the strategy independently* (Pearson & Gallagher, 1983). Various visual images for this model can be found through a simple Google search. Such skills are essential for student success on standardized tests as well as in classroom content assessments.

Before reading activities assist students in reading and understanding the text. This step is a necessary prerequisite to reader response activities. The following graphic organizer serves as a guide for students to fill out before reading nonfiction text. Students identify text features and connect their content to understanding what the nonfiction text will discuss. They also make predictions about what the text will be about. Then, after filling out the graphic organizer and subsequently reading the text, students turn their organizers over and write a brief summary of the text.

Name _____ *Date* _____

Text Feature	List Items (Include Page Number)	Purpose: How Does It Help Me Read and Understand the Information?
Table of contents		
Headings		
Bold and/or italicized words		
Graphics/picture captions/ graphs		
Index		

Before reading, complete this section: I predict this text will be about . . . _____
_____
_____
_____
_____
_____
_____

After reading the text, write a summary on the back of this paper.

Teaching *all* students to use a graphic organizer *during* reading assists them in focusing on the task at hand as well as aiding students who have memory problems. The following website has numerous content area reading graphic organizers to use *during* and *after* content area reading: http://pubs.cde.ca.gov/tcsii/ch2/scaffolding .aspx. Many different formats may be used.

Janet Allen, in her books *Reading History: A Practical Guide to Improving Literacy* (2005), *Inside Words: Tools for Teaching Academic Vocabulary Grades 4–12* (2007), and *More Tools for Teaching Content Literacy* (2008), provides teachers with graphic organizers that effectively guide students' reading with understanding, leading to the ability to successfully complete written-language reader response activities. Some students may enjoy interactive graphic organizers that can be used on their computers. Examples of these may be found at http://www.readwritethink.org/ classroom-resources/student-interactives.

Students may do the following:

- Fill out a graphic organizer for nonfiction during reading:
- What happened?
- Who was there?
- When did it happen?
- Where did it happen?
- Why did it happen?

Completing graphic organizers before and during reading gives students the background knowledge they need to comprehend what they read. Students are then able to connect prior knowledge constructions to future knowledge constructions. For teachers of English Language Learners, "activating background knowledge" often directly becomes "teaching background knowledge" due to their gaps in vocabulary knowledge. Using as many artifacts as possible to "teach" the background knowledge is important. This may involve using "hands-on" objects or valuable websites such as those of the Smithsonian at http://www.smithsonianeducation.org/educators, National Geographic at http://education.nationalgeographic.com/education/?ar_a=1, or the Environmental Protection Agency at http://www2.epa.gov/learn-issues. Filling out graphic organizers during reading gives students a visual to use after reading for their written-language reader response activities.

In this chapter, we see again that writing is intimately connected to reading. Content area teachers—that is, teachers of subjects that require content knowledge as well as skills—are more effective when they relate facts to concepts and contexts. Students remember facts that fit into their prior mental schema, and writing reinforces concept understanding. Writing should permeate the school curriculum, and students should be as likely to write in physical education classes as in English and social studies classes. A very good model for this is Brockton High School in Massachusetts. Brockton High School improved student academic performance (state test scores) by integrating writing into all subjects, even physical education (http://www.agi.harvard.edu/events/2009Conference/2009AGIConferenceReport6-30-2010web.pdf).

Content area writing positively impacts the reading/writing connection. Prior knowledge constructions are effectively expanded through written-language content area activities, thus increasing subject matter knowledge. Literacy in all cases is built and maintained through the complementary practices of reading and writing.

ACTIVITIES FOR CHAPTER 2

These activities address the Common Core Standards for reading and writing, providing teachers with a shared vision of literacy across the disciplines. The following standards in both reading and writing govern the suggested strategies that follow.

Target Anchor Standards for Reading

Standard 2. Determine central ideas or themes of a text and analyze their development; summarize the key supporting details and ideas.

Standard 3. Analyze how and why individuals, events, or ideas develop and interact over the course of a text.

Standard 7. Integrate and evaluate content presented in diverse media and formats, including visually and quantitatively, as well as the relevance and sufficiency of the evidence.

Standard 10. Read and comprehend complex literary and informational texts independently and proficiently.

Target Anchor Standards for Writing

Standard 5. Develop and strengthen writing as needed by planning, revising, editing, rewriting, or trying a new approach.

Standard 6. Use technology, including the Internet, to produce and publish writing and to interact and collaborate with others.

Standard 10. Write routinely over extended time frames (time for research, reflection, and revision) and shorter time frames (a single sitting or a day or two) for a range of tasks, purposes, and audiences.

Activity 2.1: *Using the SOAPSTone Strategy*

Learner Objective

Students identify and analyze how the context and purpose of a work impact its form and use. Teachers observe whether students are able to identify speaker, occasion, audience, purpose, subject, and tone. This activity provides a structure through which to analyze a text, eventually leading students to analyze their own written work. This can easily be applied to students' writing. How is writing a valedictory speech different from writing a sports article for the local school paper?

Assignment

Give students a few minutes to read the chosen piece. This exercise works well with the Gettysburg Address, John F. Kennedy's inaugural address, or any other primary document or speech. Read the document aloud to students, asking them to mark or note anything they "notice." Then share the acronym SOAPStone with them and together identify the context and purpose of the piece.

> *S* is for *Speaker*
> *O* is for *Occasion*
> *A* is for *Audience*
> *P* is for *Purpose*
> *S* is for *Subject*
> *Tone* is the author's attitude (ironic? flippant? angry?)

When you work your way to "tone," look to DIDLS to discern the author's attitude. How do the elements you identify contribute to your understanding of this message?

Apply SOAPSTone to a variety of genres. Find an editorial or a relevant political cartoon in the area of social studies or science. Use SOAPSTone and/or DIDLS to reveal the author's purpose.

Students Who Require Extensive Support

Students who require extensive support may use text features to show tone in their writing. Different fonts, colors, and visuals can show emotion or add voice. Visuals may be added under each sentence to increase understanding, if necessary.

> *That really HURT!*　　　*I had fun!*　　　*It was a longgggggg walk.*

Teacher Resources

The following websites offer teachers many choices to use for the SOAPStone activity:

Historical primary documents may be found at http://www.law.ou.edu/hist, http://education.nationalgeographic.com/education/media/roosevelts-day-in-famy-speech/?ar_a=1, and http://education.nationalgeographic.com/education/media/slave-sale/?ar_a=1.

Scientific primary documents may be found at http://www.loc.gov/teachers/class roommaterials/themes/science/set.html and http://guides.lib.washington.edu/content.php?pid=72468&sid=653510.

Mathematical primary documents may be found at http://education.national geographic.com/education/media/us-census-1790/?ar_a=1.

Students Who Require Extensive Support

Students who require extensive support need lots and lots of practice with all written-language concepts. One effective way to provide this practice is to teach the concepts in an interdisciplinary manner. For instance, if a particular student has a preoccupation with "peacocks," this preoccupation can be used in all disciplines. A science project can be done on the characteristics of peacocks, math word problems can be written using peacocks in the problems, a history research project can look into the history of using peacock feathers for different products, the art teacher may use pictures of peacocks to draw attention to a variety of art principles and have students write about these principles in art class, woodshop can be devoted to carving a peacock from wood and writing directions for the procedures taken, and written-language activities of all kinds can incorporate peacocks into the assignment. This provides motivation to students who have a preoccupation with a particular topic or object.

Formative Assessment

Teachers identify students' understanding of the terms *speaker, occasion, audience, purpose, subject,* and *tone.* Once students can identify these features in text, they are ready to incorporate these features into their writing. Teachers may want to introduce one feature at a time for students to include in their writing, eventually having students attempt to identify and incorporate all SOAPStone features in their own content area writing. A simple rubric can assist teachers in keeping track of students' understanding, allowing teachers to form small groups for reteaching and reinforcement of previous SOAPStone components.

Class _____ Date _____

✔+		✔				✔-	
Exemplary		*Proficient*				*Needs Improvement*	

Student Names	Content Area Understanding	S Speaker	O Occasion	A Audience	P Purpose	S Subject	T Tone

Universal Design for Learning Application

> *Engagement (stimulate interest and motivation for learning)*—Allow students to choose the topic they would like to use. Provide a choice of "topics" for those students who require more guidance.
>
> *Representation (present information and content in different ways)*—Present information using videos, recordings, images, Ted talks, and so on.
>
> *Action and expression (differentiate the ways that students can express what they know)*—Allow students to work in small groups to facilitate discussion of SOAPSTone categories, furthering concept understanding.

Activity 2.2: *Role Playing*

Learner Objective

Students explore a historical situation through writing scripts for characters. This activity requires students to understand their reading material and then write a dialogue or script demonstrating their understanding of concepts. This assists students in developing sentence fluency and voice.

Assignment

Students read to understand content area materials and then write dialogue demonstrating their understanding of concepts. This activity assists students in better comprehension of content area materials while providing written-language practice accentuating voice in writing. You are a member of the Cuban Missile Crisis Committee that President Kennedy has convened to address the Russian threat of missiles facing the United States. (http://www.smithsonianmag.com/videos/category/3play_1/historic-newsreel-footage-of-the-cuban-missi/?no-ist). Write a script for one of the people at the meeting, such as JFK's Secretary of State Dean

Rusk or Secretary of Defense Robert MacNamara; a scientist; a diplomat; or a military person. Draw from both primary and secondary sources. This writing exercise allows the students to address the research by taking on the role of a participant. Another way to role play is for students to create a travelogue in the persona of a figure living in a particular time period based on historical research.

Formative Assessment

Teachers use students' dialogue to identify students who effectively understand the content area concept as well as use the SOAPStone features. Teachers identify small groups that need to receive further instruction in any of the SOAPStone areas: speaker, occasion, audience, purpose, subject, and tone (see Activity 2.1). Teachers may do the exact same assessment using DIDLS. (See the section "Selecting Models for Reading" in chapter 1.)

Universal Design for Learning Application

Engagement (stimulate interest and motivation for learning)—Allow students to choose the work they would like to read from a list provided by the teacher after the teacher models an example.

Representation (present information and content in different ways)—Content area materials may be posters developed during a particular war or posters developed to explain a scientific principle. YouTube videos may be used for content area materials. Provide students a variety of options on their "choose from" list.

Action and expression (differentiate the ways that students can express what they know)—Allow students to demonstrate their understanding through writing by producing a cartoon strip format with dialogue clouds to demonstrate their understanding.

Activity 2.3: *Using Primary Documents*

Learner Objective

Students rewrite historical documents in their own words and voices. These activities require students to understand their reading material, demonstrating their grasp of concepts by writing in modern language. This assists students in developing sentence fluency and voice.

Assignment

Rewrite historical documents in student voice. This is a worthwhile exercise stressing literacy, while at the same time retaining the main ideas of the document. For example, take something like the Fifteenth Amendment and ask some questions to stimulate interest: "Why the Fifteenth Amendment?" Why was it necessary to create the Fifteenth Amendment to the U.S. Constitution when the Fourteenth Amendment had already provided voting rights to men? Using a variety of primary documents, such as newspaper articles, congressional reports, letters to the editor, and/or other types of primary sources, the teacher sets up an investigation for students to research and develop a report on evidence from sources and their interpretation. This activity could be used across the disciplines since it is asking students to dig deeper into knowledge through poignant, essential questions. "Why green energy?" "Of what use is algebra?"

Formative Assessment

Collect written work from students to determine document understanding as well as students' ability to insert "voice" into their writing. This will guide future lessons as well as small-group makeup.

Universal Design for Learning Application

Engagement (stimulate interest and motivation for learning)—Allow students to choose the document they would like to use for rewriting in their own voice. Provide a choice of "documents" for those students who require more guidance.

Representation (present information and content in different ways)—Present information using videos, recordings, images, YouTube videos, and so on.

Action and expression (differentiate the ways that students can express what they know)—Allow students to work in small groups to facilitate discussion of their chosen document in order to further concept understanding.

Activity 2.4: *Using Letters, Diaries, and Other Primary Sources*

Learner Objective

Students write a poem using the voice of a historical individual.

Assignment

There are collections of letters in American history as well as in a variety of world history resources. Joan Schur (2007) dedicates chapters in her book *Eyewitness to the Past* to each of these topics. She stresses taking on the *persona* of a character based on researching a specific historical figure, and she provides sources as well as examples for doing this with all students.

Getting to know a character as a person living in a specific time period encourages students to keep diary entries based on data found through the research. Reading diaries connects the student in a more personal nature with the character of a specific time period. A student could read American frontier women's diaries or the letters or diaries of Nelson Mandela, Mahatma Gandhi, Florence Nightingale, or midwives in England during World War II. Or students could delve into any diaries or letters written by members of an international nursing corps in Afghanistan or Iraq. Diaries and/or letters can also be a useful tool for students to evaluate multiple perspectives on a specific issue. Based on the reading of diaries and/or letters, have the students create the next entry in a diary based on what they have already learned about the character and of the time period (Norman & Roberts, 2013).

Formative Assessment

Teachers examine students' work to determine their understanding of the content area concept as well as their ability to express themselves clearly. Teachers check on the use of assigned readings and oral discussions and how students formulate essential questions. Checking this work will inform the teacher which students need assistance and which students can move on in the activity.

Universal Design for Learning Application

Engagement (stimulate interest and motivation for learning)—Allow students to choose the work they would like to read from a list provided by the teacher.

Representation (present information and content in different ways)—Content area materials may be posters from any era or discipline, charts, or graphs encompassing any and all content areas.

Action and expression (differentiate the ways that students can express what they know)—Allow students to demonstrate their understanding through writing by producing a cartoon strip format with dialogue clouds to demonstrate their understanding. Posters, PowerPoints, or Prezis may also allow students to demonstrate their understanding. Writing a script for a play may allow students to better demonstrate their understanding.

Activity 2.5: *Applying the Concept of Essential Questions in Content Areas*

Learner Objective

Students compose questions that transcend the specific or local text to express the bigger life questions. This activity promotes higher-level thinking skills. These questions go to the heart of the author's purpose. Promoting higher-level thinking skills aids students in better understanding texts as well as addressing these types of questions in their own writing. This brings moral and ethical concepts into the classroom.

Assignment

"Why is democracy so messy?" is a great way to introduce the realities of democratic governments and then use the text as one of your resources to investigate the issue or idea. "Are we living in a 'Gilded Age' today?" Such questions can be asked before, during, or after a lesson, allowing students to respond in writing, drawing on their own ideas based on valid and reliable sources. The Gilder Lehrman Institute (http://www.gilderlehrman.org) provides some excellent essential questions that could be used to stimulate writing. Essential questions can also be effectively used in all content areas. For example, why the zero in mathematics? How are structure and function related in living things? Review the section "Using Essential Questions" in this chapter.

Formative Assessment

The teacher examines students' work to determine if students can express abstract ideas clearly. This examination informs the teacher of student progress in writing essential questions that go beyond simple responses.

Universal Design for Learning Application

Engagement (stimulate interest and motivation for learning)—Allow students to choose from a list of essential questions brainstormed with the teacher.

Representation (present information and content in different ways)—Have students generate some visual representations of questions using a poster or electronic format.

Action and expression (differentiate the ways that students can express what they know)—Allow students to demonstrate their understanding of the essential question through some sort of visual representation, such as a poster or comic strip format. Use a "carousal activity" where students walk around the room and add their ideas to others' posters of various essential questions.

Activity 2.6: *Implementing Socratic Seminars*

Learner Objective

Students employ a discussion and subsequent writing to advance their understanding. This activity requires students to orally and subsequently in writing develop their ideas and explain their viewpoints, thus promoting clear persuasive writing.

Assignment

Socratic seminar is now a common approach to understanding ideas in many content area classrooms. This process should involve *all* students in discussing and then writing to describe what they have read or discussed from the text or from a specific reading. In this way, students draw evidence from informational texts to support analysis, reflection (Wilhelm, 2007, 2016), and research. Go to this website to find directions for using Socratic seminar for *To Kill a Mockingbird*: https://www.google .com/search?client=safari&rls=en&q=To+Kill+a+Mockingbird+Socratic+Seminar .doc&ie=UTF-8&oe=UTF-8.

Students Who Require Extensive Support

English Language Learners benefit from doing small-group work with English-proficient students. Conversations between students enhance oral language development and understanding of vocabulary and concepts in all areas. The Internet and computer afford all students acquisition of visuals to go along with new vocabulary. Websites, such as that of the Smithsonian, give students access to a wide variety of authentic artifacts to ensure understanding of a topic prior to writing about it.

Formative Assessment

Teachers examine students' work to determine how well they comprehended the reading and used the text in the follow-up discussion and in individual written work.

Universal Design for Learning Application

Engagement (stimulate interest and motivation for learning)—Allow students to choose from a list of topics provided by the teacher. Have students discuss their topic with a peer prior to the whole-class discussion.

Representation (present information and content in different ways)—Provide examples of posters, PowerPoint or other types of presentations, YouTube videos, and so on to further students' understanding of the topic and scaffold meaningful discussion if necessary with a small group.

Action and expression (differentiate the ways that students can express what they know)—Allow students to demonstrate their understanding through writing scripts for role-playing situations, producing captioned videos, or designing poster presentations. Students may choose to "write" a *Jeopardy!* game to show understanding of a content area concept.

Activity 2.7: *Reviewing the Textbook*

Learner Objective

Students apply critical analysis to textbooks and other informational text. This activity requires students to test their critical faculties by analyzing textbooks and other informational sources. Skills developed here will enhance the students' ability to write to explain informational text and write their own informational text.

Assignment

Review your textbook (specific pages or chapter) and the additional readings provided in order to respond thoughtfully to the prompt "Compare and contrast the content provided by your text and two other sources on the American labor movement:" http://www.classtools.net/education-games-php/venn_intro

What is the tone of each reading? Are the readings well written? Did each of the readings provide factual details? Did they draw from reliable and valid sources? Did they increase your learning about this time period?

Formative Assessment

Teachers examine students' work to evaluate their critical analysis of the textbooks or other informational texts, drawing on tone, writing, facts, reliability, and validity.

Universal Design for Learning Application

Engagement (stimulate interest and motivation for learning)—Allow students to choose from a list of informational texts provided by the teacher, ensuring content rigor and access.

Representation (present information and content in different ways)—Informational text may take the form of pictures, authentic documents, posters, or YouTube videos.

Action and expression (differentiate the ways that students can express what they know)—Allow students to demonstrate their understanding through developing a Venn diagram with labels.

Activity 2.8: *Journaling*

Learner Objective

Students write regularly for a specific purpose. This short activity gives students writing practice and helps them collect ideas that can be developed in the future. This is often a prewriting assignment.

Assignment

Electronic journaling may be motivating for those students who prefer using the computer for their written-language activities. Many students find electronic journaling motivating due to the fact that they can express themselves through a selection of various fonts, clip art pictures, borders, and photographs in combination with words to get their point across. As part of a science class unit on electricity, ask students to pretend they are Benjamin Franklin and have them write a letter to a colleague about the invention of the lightning rod. This will scaffold students' understanding of electricity while encouraging engagement in their learning and foster writing skills.

Try Glogster (http://edu.glogster.com/?ref=com) to help students produce interactive journals. Glogster permits students to create virtual posters using text, audio, video, images, and hyperlinks. Students share these electronically. The site allows teachers to develop class lists and monitor student work while protecting privacy and anonymity. There is a cost for using this Web 2.0 tool; however, students can produce their own videos, audios, and other visuals to demonstrate their knowledge.

Formative Assessment

Teachers read students' ongoing journal entries to look for patterns, ideas, and use of media as well as to offer suggestions for further readings.

Universal Design for Learning Application

> *Engagement (stimulate interest and motivation for learning)*—The teacher chooses a relevant engaging topic: for example, a current headline from the news or a choice of one or two engaging quotations.
>
> *Representation (present information and content in different ways)*—Students could illustrate in their journals some visual representation using labeled posters or pictures. This could also be done on the computer.
>
> *Action and expression (differentiate the ways that students can express what they know)*—Allow students to demonstrate their understanding through the above.

Activity 2.9: *Authentic Content Area Writing*

Learner Objective

Students write to communicate information and ideas to others. This authentic writing activity promotes clear, concise writing, often increasing cultural understandings.

Assignment

Students can be motivated by communicating with students from other countries. This communication effectively engages students in the writing process and can be used to increase comprehension in any content area while improving and practicing written-language skills. Classrooms may choose to use the ePals website (http://www .epals.com). Sign up for a free account and discover the vast number of free activities offered to educators and students alike.

For example, have students tell their e-pals about the geography of the area where they live. Perhaps students would like to describe local landmarks. These landmarks may encompass monuments, rivers, mountains, or other physical land features. Students describe the landmark and where it is located as well as what it tells them about history. Students may hone their geography skills through rich, accurate descriptions of the landmarks. Pictures with captions may be utilized to further extend the understanding for their e-pals.

Students will have to answer questions posed by their e-pals after reading the descriptions. This reinforces students' learning to write clearly. Having to explain specific content area learnings through writing reinforces understanding by the writer. Students can explain a recently conducted science experiment or mathematical concept or operation learned in class. Students from one country find it fascinating to learn about what their peers are doing in another country. Make sure that you communicate with a class that is committed to agreed-on time lines and communication dates. Also, make sure both classes know about each other's vacation times! (Charron, 2007).

Formative Assessment

Teachers examine students' letters to determine specifically where each individual student needs to improve in his or her writing. Teachers conference with individual students or small groups in the area of need.

Universal Design for Learning Application

Engagement (stimulate interest and motivation for learning)—Allow students to choose what topics they would like to communicate with their e-pals about.

Representation (present information and content in different ways)—Allow students to utilize a variety of fonts, borders, and pictures to communicate ideas to their e-pals.

Action and expression (differentiate the ways that students can express what they know)—Allow students to demonstrate their effective communication through a selection of various fonts, clip art pictures, borders, and photographs in combination with words to get their point across. PowerPoints, Prezis, comic strips, and captioned videos may be used. The possibilities are endless.

3

Developing Focus and Logic through the Essay

The essay is a literary device for saying almost everything about almost anything.

—Aldous Huxley

As modern educators understand it, an essay is a personal statement of some import, usually short, that puts forth an idea and supports that idea through various kinds of evidence. Although the essay may truly encompass many topics in many disparate ways, it is the darling of modern education for good reason. Students learn to present an individual point of view in writing, ranging from the personal to the abstract, depending on the essay's purpose. Persuasive skills are inherent to the essay and are necessities for lifelong writing. Focus and logic are prerequisites to successful argument.

Huxley (1959) calls these various purposes a "three-poled frame of reference." He tells us that an essay can be *intensely individual,* based on memoir or other personal experience; it can present a *point of view* about anything factual or objective; or it can be *totally abstract,* the fleshing out of a concept. Huxley argues that an essay may call on all three worlds. In fact, however, when a teacher asks students to write an essay, the hope is that their product will competently address any *one* of these.

Educators prize the essay because it asks students to demonstrate a fairly high level of organizational skill in stating their main idea, in supporting that idea with evidence, and in marshaling material to make each point. They must focus. They must prioritize. They must execute with clarity. These are the academic skills they will need to be successful in college and in life. Although they may never write another formal academic essay in their lives, they will use their skills to be successful in whatever they do: they will need to discern what is important, to reformulate what they know or what they think to accomplish, and to present that purposeful statement in order to sway others to their view.

USING MODELS OF ESSAY WRITING

The question, therefore, is this: How can teachers use the essay to instruct students how to think well and express their ideas for maximum effect? In other words, if the essay is a vehicle for education, which it seems to be, then how can teachers use it to enhance students' skills both in writing and in critical thinking?

As always, reading and analyzing effective essays are valuable experiences. Models of good writing are worthy of study. To teach a student how to write an "A" paper, wouldn't it be reasonable to let the student read a few "A" papers?

A most instructive essay model, which actually covers all three of Huxley's poles, is E. B. White's classic personal essay "Once More to the Lake." From White, students can learn how to weave a theme or key word throughout a piece of writing for effect, however subtle. It is a masterpiece of form supporting meaning, as the repetition of words, phrases, and images mimics the meaning.

The essay *is* its main idea. One could get dizzy right along with E. B. White, matching the similarities and differences, past and present, father and son. Suddenly, the reader is the central figure, regardless of age, watching and participating in the progression of the generations. White mesmerizes readers with a timeless idea, and with him readers recognize their humanity and their mortality. Any single paragraph will illustrate this point. Find the line or sentence that best captures it. Underline it. Once you, the reader, map the repetitions, the meaning reveals itself. (See Activity 3.1: *How Meaning Is Constructed in E. B. White's "Once More to the Lake,"* http://wheretheclassroomends.com/wp-content/uploads/2013/07/White_OnceMoreto theLake1.pdf.)

USING ESSENTIAL QUESTIONS IN ESSAY WRITING

An essential question is a life question, a question to which all human beings (or at least a subgroup of all human beings) would seek the answer. For example, an essential question behind White's "Once More to the Lake" might be the life question, "How do the details of everyday life reveal the larger truths of Life? " or "Why or how is the passage of time part of the experience of being human?"

Essays often have a thesis statement prominently positioned. White's point is subtle such that the last sentence of the essay catches the reader by surprise. The essay may answer an essential question, but the answer is never definitive because the essay provides *an* answer, not *the* answer. Other questions: What is the nature of memory? Can memory capture reality? Over time, what is real? Is life merely a prelude to death? Generating essential questions from reading is a higher-level thinking skill that prepares writers to plan how they will build around an idea or purpose that they have for their own writing.

Annie Dillard's (1987) excellent piece, excerpted from *An American Childhood*, is widely used in classrooms. It is popular with students because most children in northern America have launched a snowball at a car. Dillard's story serves a point, so it can be said to be an essay illustrated by a narrative. No essential question can be answered from only one work, but the essential questions underlying this narrative include "What is the attraction of breaking rules? and "How do children challenge adult authority?" Or a question could be stated, "What is the premier prerequisite for success?" Identifying the thesis in the piece provides a potential answer.

Answers simply provide evidence, one way or the other. (See Activity 3.2: *Form Supports Meaning.*)

Every essay should generate its own essential question and could certainly have more than one. This is the process of determining the focus of a piece. This is where the "engine" of an essay lies. What drives it? What do human beings seek? What small potential piece of the puzzle of life does this work offer? Questions are far more important than answers.

In our cultural diversity, we may find many disparate answers, but our questions are the same because we are all human. Push students to formulate questions that are truly "essential." For students who find it difficult to think in terms of essential questions, a more accessible strategy might be to capture the main idea through theme identification, which is rooted in the story line. Theme is local to the story, whereas essential questions are life questions. (See Activity 3.3: *Conversion of a Narrative to an Essay.*)

WRITING ESSAYS ABOUT LITERATURE

In *Death of a Salesman*, what is the *significance* of Willy's insurance policy? In Curtis's *Bud, Not Buddy*, what is the *significance* of Bud's suitcase? In the student's essay, what is the *significance* of the setting? Determining significance is actually evaluative in Bloom's spectrum of thinking or questioning (see the section "It Helps to Ask the Right Question!" in chapter 1). Encourage students to accept the challenge of articulating significance. Through articulating significance, students bring focus and logic to their writing.

The value of this type of activity is to launch our discussion of literature into the larger human meaning. *My* mother becomes an essay about mothers. *My* teacher becomes an essay about teachers or teaching. *My* summer (like E. B. White's) becomes a summer of significance for all Americans or at least for those who have a pattern, generation to generation or summer after summer, whatever that pattern may be.

A student is given a task of writing about a person. The student chooses his best friend Joe. Why Joe? What about Joe makes him worth writing about? By asking probing questions, we lead the student to identify the significance of choosing Joe. Perhaps this is an essay about best friends. Probing questions may scaffold students' thinking. Somewhere in that narrative is its significance to that student. We can help students find the essential questions that drive them to capture their experiences in writing. (See Activity 3.4: *Finding Significance in Literature.*)

WRITING ESSAYS IN THE CONTENT AREAS

As we indicated in chapter 2, discussing the success of Brockton High School, writing should permeate the school curriculum, as there are arguments to be had and ideas to present in all subjects—math and science as well as social studies and English—and students should be as likely to write in physical education classes as in English and social studies classes. Brockton High School improved student academic performance (state test scores) by integrating writing into all subjects, even physical education. By writing in the content areas, students become familiar with the vocabulary of their specific content areas and learn practical strategies to access that content (Fang, 2014).

Why essay writing? Traditionally, students have written "reports." A report is what its name says: it is simply a write-up of what the student found out. Often, students write reports with no critical consideration of the issue and no reasoned opinion. A report has no engine. An essay, however, has a point. The audience of an essay needs to be persuaded to the writer's idea. Evidence must be presented. If we seek to raise the level of critical thinking in our students, we need to raise the bar (Milo, 2017). Encourage students to interact with their subject. An essay can evolve from a story, a narrative, a letter to the editor, an oral history, or a diary entry and then be polished into a persuasive/reflective essay.

Students could write essays to develop a newspaper on the American Revolution that presents multiple viewpoints on the ideology of the revolution. Essays on World War II could take the form of letters, both pro and con, written to officials on various topics, such as the expression of a Japanese American's viewpoint, of a conscientious objector, or of an advocate of Charles Lindbergh's isolationism. Why not write about the moral imperative of the dropping of the A-bomb in health and in social studies? The goal, as stated earlier, is "to launch our discussion into the larger human meaning."

Essential questions that may inspire essays include "Why revolution?" or "Is revolution an evolving idea?," "Why war?," and "How is mathematics useful to people's lives?" These are the bigger questions that rely on knowledge of content and critical thinking and that could have been written first as journal entries and then developed into formal essays. Writing down our questions helps us to put our learning into context. It helps us to develop a hypothesis. It supports our thinking as we use logic to develop, express, and defend our ideas. (See Activity 3.5: *Brainstorming in Response to Essential Questions.*)

The next chapter discusses writing specifically for persuasive purposes. Essay writing skills are fundamental to understanding argument and its requirements bridging to the Common Core Standards.

ACTIVITIES FOR CHAPTER 3

These activities address the Common Core Standards for reading and writing, providing teachers with a shared vision of literacy across the disciplines. The following standards in both reading and writing govern the suggested strategies that follow.

Target Anchor Standards for Reading

Standard 4. Interpret words and phrases as they are used in the text, including determining technical, connotative, and figurative meanings, and analyze how specific word choices shape meaning or tone.

Standard 6. Assess how point of view or purpose shapes the content and style of a text.

Target Anchor Standards for Writing

Standard 3. Write narratives to develop real or imagined experiences or events using effective technique, well-chosen details, and well-structured event sequences.

Activity 3.1: *How Meaning Is Constructed in E. B. White's "Once More to the Lake"*

Learner Objective

Students closely read examples of excellent essays to determine how meaning is constructed. This activity guides students in identifying the particulars of what a skilled writer does. Noticing the repetition of words in this personal essay offers a choice to a prospective writer. Repetition here is deliberate, not accidental.

Assignment

First, have students work in pairs to draw lines on their copy between White's many twin expressions. Watch for repetition in this piece. Mark it up by circling words and phrases that repeat and draw a line between them. Help students articulate how meaning is constructed in White's piece to explain how this writing strategy mimics the point. *Form supports meaning.*

Students Who Require Extensive Support

Students who require extensive support will need access to pages that aid them with an explanation of language arts vocabulary. They will require frequent access to their language arts notebook for future access to vocabulary. Students may also benefit by planning writing their essay using this website: http://www.readwritethink.org/classroom-resources/student-interactives/essay-30063.html

The chart below is a good way to increase understanding of the different types of essays. Clip art pictures may be added to each section to promote understanding.

Personal Essay	Factual Essay	Abstract Essay
Choose a person.	Choose a holiday.	Choose a concept, such as friendship or courage.
Write one page about this person.	Write one page about the holiday.	Write one page on the concept.
Why did you choose this person?	Why is this holiday significant?	Why is this concept significant?
I wrote about _____ because _____.	This holiday is important because _____.	This concept is important because _____.

Next, have students determine the "thesis statement" or main idea of this essay. Have them find the line or the sentence that best captures it, then underline it. Once students map the repetitions, the meaning reveals itself.

Students Who Require Extensive Support

Students who require extensive support need to work with text at their instructional level and underline the sentence that best expresses the main idea.

Formative Assessment

The teacher invites students to compare marked-up texts and discuss and write reasons for the repetition, guiding them to make suppositions. Teachers may examine student work to track students' understandings and guide future lessons.

Universal Design for Learning Application

Engagement (stimulate interest and motivation for learning)—Allow students to choose the essay they would like to read from a list provided by the teacher.

Representation (present information and content in different ways)—Provide a variety
of genres for students to choose from.

*Action and expression (differentiate the ways that students can express what they
know)*—Allow students to make a list of what they notice.

Activity 3.2: *Form Supports Meaning*

Learner Objective

Students will find examples of DIDLS in an effective personal essay and show how
a writer uses the elements to reinforce the main idea. This activity is a precursor to
students writing their own personal essays. Students use the examples from Dillard's
personal essay to improve the writing of their own essays.

Assignment

Find the segment in Annie Dillard's *An American Childhood* (http://wiki.theplaz
.com/w/images/6-Getting_Caught_Reading.pdf) that tells about throwing snow-
balls at cars. Have students read it individually. Then read it out loud to them as
they mark what they see and hear and what they like or notice, whether well-chosen
words, images, details, a type of language (religious?), or syntax. What was particularly effective? Students can choose one element (DIDLS) to write about. How did
diction (imagery, detail, language, or syntax) help to make this personal essay effective? On which of these elements does the author rely most to convey her point?
Students can be invited to draw the images brought to mind in reading Dillard's
piece. A list of sensory images could be categorized and listed.

Students Who Require Extensive Support

Students who require extensive support require explicit instruction of language
arts vocabulary. Providing students the below visual structure, provides them
access to language arts vocabulary. Color coding may increase access to this
understanding. Visuals such as clip art or photographs may be added to further
enhance comprehension. As always, include the chart below in the student's
language arts notebook for future use. Clip art pictures may be added to each
section to promote understanding.

Diction	Imagery	Detail	Language/Syntax
Word choice: meander or walk?	Picture in head	Specifics	Wow! What a hit!
	The *white lacy delicate* flower.	The boy hit the ball, rounded first, and slid into second base.	

Formative Assessment

Students will catalog the examples of *diction, imagery, detail, language,* and *syntax.* Teachers will review their categorization to ensure that students applied the terms correctly.

Summative Assessment

Students choose one element and write how the author develops meaning through the element. Understanding this concept may then be transferred to students' own writing.

Universal Design for Learning Application

   Engagement (stimulate interest and motivation for learning)—Allow students to choose a partner to work with to discuss Dillard's essay.
   Representation (present information and content in different ways)—Provide a recording of the passage for students to listen to before the lesson is taught in the classroom. Ensure understanding of literary terms prior to listening to the tape (see text box above).
   Action and expression (differentiate the ways that students can express what they know)—Allow students to demonstrate their understanding through discussing information with a partner. Provide a checklist for them to "check off" and record the literary elements they find.

Activity 3.3: *Conversion of a Narrative to an Essay*

Learner Objective

Students write to develop their own narratives from childhood experiences and then develop a thesis statement that expresses the significance of the event. This activity promotes critical thinking and writing by having students formulate a statement that expresses the essential meaning of an event.

Assignments

Have students begin by telling a story of something that happened in their lives. Or they can begin by writing about an event, a person, a place, or an object. Once the descriptive/narrative is complete, they will use it as the basis for the following assignment. Have students consider why they chose this event, person, place, or object. In its significance is its larger meaning. If students are writing about a person, have them explain why that person was chosen. If they chose a place, why was that place significant in their lives? Identifying the significance of something is a higher-level thinking activity. It is to find the thesis or engine for an essay. Help students consider

Students Who Require Extensive Support

Students who require extensive support need direct instruction in understanding voice with numerous examples provided and lots of practice in both real-life settings and during writing instruction. Start by providing students with examples of using voice in writing using simple vocabulary, short sentences, and complementary punctuation. Include these examples in the student's writing notebook. Photographs with the student in them are a motivating way to teach voice. Clip art pictures may be added to each section to promote understanding.

Weak Voice	Strong Voice
I had fun.	Wow! What fun!

thesis statements that will capture that significance.

Summative Assessment

The teacher conferences with a student to scaffold the student's discovery of the essential meaning. The teacher helps the student bridge the narrative with the essay. The summative assessment should include approval of the student's thesis statement.

Universal Design for Learning Application (http://www.cast.org)

Engagement (stimulate interest and motivation for learning)—Students will already be engaged in this activity as they are using personal experiences.

Representation (present information and content in different ways)—The teacher can model this activity using his or her own personal experience.

Action and expression (differentiate the ways that students can express what they know)—Allow students to demonstrate their understanding through writing by producing PowerPoints or Prezis or producing a project-based demonstration of knowledge, possibly a visual poster. Some students may want to write from a personal photograph or bring in a family picture album. Picture captions may guide students' thinking for their thesis statement.

Activity 3.4: *Finding Significance in Literature*

Learner Objective

Students recognize and explain the significance of objects or their descriptions (detail) found in reading. This activity often involves conversations about symbolism. After students identify significant objects or details in reading, they will be ready to add the "telling detail" in their own writing.

Assignment

When reading a novel or short story, keep a written inventory of objects or interesting details and try to capture their significance to the story:

* In Pam Muñoz Ryan's *Esperanza Rising* (2000), trace the significance of fruit. Write a paragraph exploring fruit as a theme and as a symbol. What other objects have significance in that novel? How can you document "significance" with textual evidence?
* In Christopher Paul Curtis's *Bud, Not Buddy* (1999), find significance in Bud's suitcase—and in other various boxes and containers included in this young adult novel.
* In Arthur Miller's *Death of a Salesman* (1971), what is the significance of the mortgage?
* Or analyze the significance of setting in any novel or play or analyze the presence of a minor character.

Formative Assessment

Teacher reviews students' lists of significant details and their intentions to determine future teachings. Is it a symbol as well as a detail?

Universal Design for Learning Application (http://www.cast.org)

> *Engagement (stimulate interest and motivation for learning)*—Allow students to choose the story they would like to use for this activity. The teacher may want to provide the student with a "choice list" of stories that he or she knows the student comprehends for this activity. Fairy tales and fables are often well known to students.
>
> *Representation (present information and content in different ways)*—The teacher can model this activity by using a story familiar to all. Refer to the text box above for possible visual representations of presented material.

Students Who Require Extensive Support

Use a familiar story, fable, or fairy tale(s) to understand what the term *theme* means. Using visuals from a book or other source, review an already *well-known* story with the student. Have the student demonstrate understanding of the story. This may involve the student retelling the story, arranging pictures depicting the story in the correct order, or drawing the story sequentially using comic strip squares. Then ensure that the student understands the *significance of various details* of the story. Several examples may need to be provided. Putting samples in the student's language arts notebook will allow for easy review as necessary. Clip art pictures may be added to each section to promote understanding.

Cinderella

Cinderella's father dies, and her mean stepmother and stepsisters treat her like a servant. She is dressed in rags.	A magic fairy changes Cinderella's rags into a beautiful gown and slippers. She turns pumpkins into a coach and mice into horses.	Cinderella looks pretty in her new clothes.	Cinderella goes to the ball (dance), dances with the prince, but loses her slipper when she runs to go home at midnight.
Cinderella needs and deserves someone to help her.	*She gains a magical helper.*	*She looks the part.*	*She leaves a clue that she is the right one.*

At midnight, the coach changes back into a pumpkin, and the horses change back into mice. Cinderella went back to the mean stepmother's house, and her clothes changed back to rags.	The prince took the glass slipper and had different women try it on to find out to whom it belonged. He went to the mean stepmother's house. The mean stepsisters tried on the slipper. It did *not* fit. Cinderella tried the slipper. The slipper fit perfectly on Cinderella's foot. The prince realized that Cinderella was the girl he danced with at the ball! He loved Cinderella.	Cinderella and the prince married, and they lived happily ever after.
Back to reality.	*The prince recognizes she is the one.*	*Deserving people get what they deserve.*

Conclusion: Deserving people get what they deserve!

Action and expression (differentiate the ways that students can express what they know)—Allow students to demonstrate their understanding through small-group discussions and reporting to the class.

Activity 3.5: *Brainstorming in Response to Essential Questions*

Learner Objective

Students create a list of possible answers that address essential questions that focus on a content area essay idea. This prewriting activity is a higher-level thinking exercise in identifying meaning or significance that will scaffold the formation of thesis statements. This activity prepares a writer to develop and organize material around content area ideas. This might be followed by an organizer or outline of the ideas.

Assignment

Ask students to brainstorm potential answers to essential questions in the content areas.

- How does the environment shape human activity? (science)
- What do numbers mean? (mathematics)
- Is revolution an evolving idea? (history)
- How does language change in response to change in society? (language arts)
- How can one express complex ideas in simple terms? (all subjects)

Formative Assessment

The teacher reviews students' organizers/outlines to determine if students are ready to write the essay.

Universal Design for Learning Application

Engagement (stimulate interest and motivation for learning)—Allow students to work in small groups, allowing for lots of discussion.

Representation (present information and content in different ways)—Provide a variety of genres for students to choose questions from. Newspaper articles or relevant political cartoons in the area of social studies, mathematics, or science may be a possibility.

Action and expression (differentiate the ways that students can express what they know)—Allow students to demonstrate their understanding through writing by producing PowerPoints or Prezis or producing a project-based demonstration of knowledge, possibly a propaganda or election visual poster or comic strip representation of their understanding. A student may enjoy writing an editorial in response to the essential question.

4

Reading for Persuasive Writing

The Argument

To be persuasive we must be believable; to be believable we must be credible; credible we must be truthful.

—Edward R. Murrow

According to the Common Core State Standards Initiative (CCSSI) in the document titled "Key Shifts in English Language Arts" (http://www.corestandards.org/other.../key-shifts-in-english-language-arts),

> Though the standards (Common Core) still expect narrative writing throughout the grades, they also expect a command of sequence and detail that are essential for effective argumentative and informative writing. The Standards focus on evidence-based writing along with the ability to inform and persuade and is a significant shift from current practice.

There comes a time in life when one has to step up and persuade others to one's side. A wrong needs to be made right. Someone needs to come forward and take the lead, and you are that person. The virtue of one's opinion or the benefit of a certain way of doing something must be communicated and argued.

In both the professional world and the personal world, people need to articulate and defend their positions. A course of action is recommended, a product unveiled, or a person or position advocated. The need for argument is felt in the personal world as well. Why do I deserve a raise? Why should my child be promoted or rewarded? Why is it desirable to buy that new car or house?

In the school setting, however, motivation is often more difficult to come by, and most papers are mere academic exercises. Students hone their skills, and we, their teachers, try to simulate situations worth the argument. They joust, anticipating a larger arena somewhere in the future. It has been argued by some that we need to ignite their passions by adopting social issues that we educators often care about more than they.

The problem is how to motivate. How do teachers motivate students to get involved and to care about an issue, to investigate it, and to find evidence to support the argument? Educational research tells us that teacher involvement, appropriate challenge level, clearly stated learning goals, clear feedback, student choice, collaboration, effective strategy instruction, and relevance to students' interests and lives encompassing real-life interactions are crucial for student engagement (Allington, 2011; Guthrie & Klauda, 2014; Guthrie, McRae, & Klauda, 2007; Guthrie, Wigfield, & VonSecker, 2000; Guthrie et al., 2006; National Research Council, 2004; Robertson, Ford-Connors, & Dougherty, 2017; Schunk, 2003; Schunk & Rice, 1993).

According to the CCSSI,

> The Common Core emphasizes using evidence from texts to present careful analyses, well-defended claims, and clear information. Rather than asking students questions they can answer solely from their prior knowledge and experience, the standards call for students to answer questions that depend on their having read the texts with care. ("Key Shifts in English Language Arts")

As educators, we believe that offering a variety of choices for students helps to motivate many of them. Activities for this chapter are designed specifically to engage and motivate. Each activity has elements of choice or personal investment built in. Taking time to individualize some choices and offering support to students investigating their chosen topic will further engage students. Sometimes, working out individual contracts with concrete incentives may also help. Finally, for those hard-core students for whom nothing seems to work, why not investigate their interests in their content area classes? Taking time to talk one to one with students may glean information that could help students formulate a better choice. As students often say, "Keep it real"—or, in educational terms, "authentic."

FINDING "AUTHENTIC" ISSUES

Rather than feeding students a stream of worn-out issues from a list, let's help students find their own issues, do research to educate themselves, and then argue *their* ideas, not those of their parents and certainly not ours. Too many students are led down the garden path to the preferences and opinions of adults, which we make all too clear for them.

The authors of the Common Core Standards advocate that students are ready to argue for their own opinions, but let's face it: some students do not have enough world knowledge or experience at this stage of their education to strike off on their own on national or global issues. Middle schoolers, for example, can be both knowledgeable and passionate about their local issues: adding a candy machine or a soda machine to the cafeteria or allowing students' input into determining a dress code.

Some issues may be personal, like the Fourth Amendment argument, "You can't search my locker and you didn't have 'probable cause,' so I shouldn't be expelled for drugs" or "You can't prevent me from voting in the school election just because I swore at a teacher." Students are motivated to research and learn about such issues, and it is important that they *read* the law both for their information *and* for their better literacy. With the perennial issues of capital punishment, abortion, and legalization of marijuana, we can, as Vygotsky (1997) advocated, help them read up, study the issues, and work to stretch to their highest developmental potential, but arguing for these is unlikely to sway an audience, and the path is so well traveled that the argument becomes predictable and easily borrowed from digital sources.

All students are capable of finding authentic topics by reading news or magazine articles and then working to identify the position of the journalist or newspaper. They can compare positions among writers/papers on the same topics, and they can find quotes that support their discussion (Common Core Anchor Standards 8 and 9). The skills that are built in the activities in chapters 1 and 2, especially those dealing with diction and details, are applicable here.

Kelly Gallagher (2009, 2011) suggests taking time out of English class in high school to read and discuss an article each week in order to improve the students' background knowledge. Without general background knowledge, the high school writer is irresponsible in writing an opinion! This practice will also be motivational because the students will become familiar with various voices and stances around which they may frame an argument later (Monahan, 2013). Even though traditional journalism purports to present the facts of a matter, each article has a perspective, and the expected emotional response of the reader is implied. Close reading of nonfiction texts, using strategies for detecting tone, will help students discern the attitude and intent of the writer. The Common Core emphasizes the reading of nonfiction text:

CCSSS.ELA-LITERACY.CCRA.RI: Read closely to determine what the text says explicitly and to make logical inferences from it; cite specific textual evidence when writing or speaking to support conclusions drawn from the text.

Such readings build both knowledge and skill. For a further explanation of close reading, see chapter 1, "Close Reading: Noticing Writers' Choices." Further, we need to understand the word *text* to encompass a variety of written sources, far beyond what is in a textbook. Expand the definition of text for students to include magazines, newspapers, periodicals, and online sources, among others.

Detecting the attitude of a writer is key to knowing what he or she wants from the reader. Students need to analyze the diction and the details of the article or argument as well as the quality of evidence offered in its support. In reading carefully, they will see that each word conveys an attitude as well as a meaning. *There is no writing that is devoid of tone.*

In order to support students in this critical thinking, we create templates that help students read more carefully and organize their thinking.

Students Who Require Extensive Support

Students who require extensive support may benefit from a graphic organizer to guide their thinking. Students identified with attention-deficit/hyperactivity disorder (ADHD) will benefit from the organizational features of a template as well as have their attention focused on the correct material. Students with communication disorders or students with autism will also benefit from having a visual reinforcing the teacher's verbal directions. English Language Learners profit from having clear visual directions. Adding a visual template provides access so that all students can complete the task successfully.

Include some of the following:

- The author wants me to _____. I know this because _____.

- The author wants me to feel _____. I know this because _____.

- List the merits of this article/argument. (Why should I do or feel these things?)

List any weaknesses you see in this author's article/argument. Is this author's position convincing?

CLOSE READING THE STRUCTURE OF AN ARGUMENT

Read before writing! Let's look at the logic and structure of good writing models before attempting to write. Have students study the overall structural plan of an article, editorial, review, or other argument. Keep high-quality reading materials at hand so that students have good options for study. Keep students motivated with material that interests them. Make sure the arguments they are asked to write align with their personal interests or preferences. In science class, students can research a controversial topic and write an argument, either pro or con, on the controversy. High-quality reading in science, as in other content areas, provides the background and the issues that are the basis for many of today's arguments. Sports provide high-interest topics, accessible on the sports pages of the local newspaper.

How does one "close read" a model for writing? (see Activity 4.1: *Checklist for Close Reading*). Begin by asking students to give the title their attention. What do they expect after reading the title? Does the piece have a subtitle? If so, what is the relationship between the title and the subtitle? By analyzing headlines and subtitles, students can identify the leading ideas. Where is the article placed in the newspaper or magazine? How does its position in the paper or on the page reveal the opinion of the editors?

What determines the order of the information in the article? What is the lead sentence? A good article tries to give the reader a reason to continue. What is the "hook"? A newspaper article usually gives information in descending importance so that the reader can efficiently catch the major points without necessarily reading the whole article. A magazine article may withhold some information to invite the reader to continue to read to the end.

An argument is organized for its own purposes. *Where* does a writer place the most important points in the course of the argument? What is the logical flow of the argument? Students can study the various ways in which good writers transition from one point to the next in their paragraphing. What words help the reader follow the argument? Offer students a list of common transitional devices (http://www.smart -words.org/linking-words/transition-words.html). Does the word *but* or *however* occur? Help them map the logical structure and determine the most advantageous placement of these devices.

Does the author of the article include any contradictory evidence? Does he or she make any concessions to opposing arguments? Where in the development of the argument is contradictory evidence positioned? Discuss the strategy of the writer. Approaching a written piece this way allows the student to actively grapple with the piece in an attempt to ascertain the choices the writer made in crafting it. It requires inference (See Activity 5.10 in chapter 5 for students who require extensive support.) It is not simply a matter of comprehension. The reader needs to delve into the article to critically evaluate its import. Is there anything left out that you, the reader, would like to know? Follow up the topic by monitoring editorials for the next few days. By seeking the answers to these questions, we can help the student gauge the writer's position on a topic.

Next, have students look for repetition of words or phrases. How can strategic repetition strengthen the logical flow? How much repetition is too much? In their own writing, have students experiment with planting key words or phrases in multiple paragraphs. An echo can be very effective, even when not noticed by the reader. In chapter 3, we noticed how E. B. White skillfully used repetition in his personal essay "Once More to the Lake." Now notice how this device is employed in Lincoln's Gettysburg Address, which is an argument as well as an inspirational speech. Map out the words that are repeated. Notice the progression of thought with the word *Now* that begins paragraph 2. Also notice how the word *But* in paragraph 3 pivots the direction of the argument.

Students should look at the various effects of syntax in the articles and arguments read as a class. Notice passive constructions and decide whether they are effective (and some are!). Think of possible reasons they might be used for deliberate effect.

When are longer sentences most effective? When is the creation of a list in writing useful? The Declaration of Independence, for example, is an argument that makes use of a list of reasons for proposing separation from England. Similarly, in Martin Luther King's "Letter from Birmingham Jail," he creates a very long sentence listing injustices that need to be addressed. Why are very long sentences and paragraphs useful for their purposes?

When students write to argue, they should be mindful of their sentence structure. Which constructions do they tend to favor? Do they have a tendency to stick to simple sentences? Compound sentences? It is often useful to have students look at past work (not recent work) to study their own writing. Have students keep track of what they notice.

What is the purpose of a rhetorical question? Find an argument that makes use of this device and decide whether and when it might be useful. Explore the usefulness of an appositive (a word or phrase that restates or redefines what came before it) and try it out. Read a powerful argument and evaluate choices of syntax. Why are longer and more complex sentences used so often in argument? What value might there be in alternating sentence length? Experiment with shifting from active to passive voice. How does that change the ebb and flow of the energy? Which is more compelling? A link for websites on active versus passive voice can be located at https://www.google.com/search?q=passive+vs.+active+voice&ie=utf-8&oe=utf-8#q=passive+vs.+active+voice+for+elementary+school.

An argument is more than a logical discussion. It is a work crafted by a writer for a persuasive purpose. The choices available to a writer are no less strategic than if that writer were crafting a poem! The close reading of others' masterful arguments provides us with a tutorial for writing persuasively and well.

LITERARY ARGUMENTS

In literature, we also encounter argument. In writing about literature, we put forth our opinions supported by textual evidence, using the same skills we would in writing any argument. Andrew Marvell's poem "To His Coy Mistress" is an argument that makes interesting use of transitions to signal the logical shift. *Carpe diem* is itself an argument! Such poems are wonderful fun for high school students on Valentine's Day, when little else will hold their interest. Sonnets often have argumentative structures. Spencer has a number of sonnets that are well-structured arguments. Jonathan Swift's "A Modest Proposal" is a favorite in high school. His satire is well deserving of close reading.

What other punctuation does the writer have besides the usual commas and periods? What is the virtue of a semicolon? A colon? A dash? Consult Andrew Marvell! Have students choose sentences from their reading with marks of punctuation that they think are effective or sentences that are deliberately constructed for effect. Have them explain their choices by writing, as preliminary to pointing out the sentences to the class and describing how they think their chosen sentences work. Have students notice and describe the energy and the action of a sentence, which are so important in argumentation. Where might a person be convinced? Building better sentences and paragraphs is essential to getting one's good idea on its way!

A CLOSING ARGUMENT ON ARGUMENTS

The activities appended to this chapter are motivating and of minimal risk to the student. These approaches build skills and engagement. They invite participation and prepare students to write persuasively. It will be helpful to have students take a minute to write down their thoughts and opinions every time the class prepares to share their thoughts so that everyone has a ready contribution to discussion. Sharing with a neighbor to solicit feedback further confirms for the student that it is safe to share his or her thoughts with the whole class.

Activities 4.2 to 4.5 have strong oral components that help build the logic and strength of arguments. Activity 4.2: *The Face-Off* frames out an argument and helps the entire class understand both sides of an issue before forming their own opinions. Activity 4.3: *The Scaffolded Oral Presentation* puts the emphasis on reading and interpreting written arguments, gradually increasing the difficulty from one task to the next. This could be done for the benefit of honing public speaking skills, or it could culminate in three pieces of writing. Both the Activity 4.4: *A Panel Discussion* and Activity 4.5: *Staging the Trial* are dramatic presentations of points of view of characters whose personas students can adopt. The challenge comes with students extrapolating the point of view of their character from their reading and study of the character.

Finally, Activity 4.6: *Defending Preference* asks students to research a number of opinions and then choose two whose views seem most logical and persuasive. The student argues for the positions that make the most sense to him or her. All these activities offer opportunities for creative and critical engagement. All offer support for every student's full participation and benefit.

Powerful thoughts and opinions demand that words work hard to sweep the reader up with the force and energy of language, recognizing that every position we take is actually an argument.

Students Who Require Extensive Support

Students' thinking may be supported by the many graphic organizers and templates presented in this chapter. Some general education students, many students with special needs, as well as English Language Learners benefit from using graphic organizers to guide their critical thinking and subsequent writing.

ACTIVITIES FOR CHAPTER 4

These activities address the Common Core Standards for reading and writing, providing teachers with a shared vision of literacy across the disciplines. The following standards in both reading and writing govern the suggested strategies that follow.

Target Anchor Reading Standards

Standard 8. Delineate and evaluate the argument and specific claims in a text, including the validity of the reasoning as well as the relevance and sufficiency of the evidence.

Standard 9. Analyze how two or more texts address similar themes or topics in order to build knowledge or to compare the approaches the authors take.

Target Anchor Writing Standards

Standard 1. Write arguments to support claims in an analysis of substantive topics or texts using valid reasoning and relevant and sufficient evidence.

Standard 2. Write informative/explanatory texts to examine and convey complex ideas and information clearly and accurately through the effective selection, organization, and analysis of content.

Standard 7. Conduct short as well as more sustained research projects to answer a question (including a self-generated question) or solve a problem; narrow or broaden the inquiry when appropriate; synthesize multiple sources on the subject, demonstrating understanding of the subject under investigation.

Standard 8. Gather relevant information from multiple authoritative print and digital sources, using advanced searches effectively; assess the usefulness of each source in answering the research question; integrate information into the text selectively to maintain the flow of ideas, avoiding plagiarism and following standard format for citation.

Standard 9. Draw evidence from informational texts to support analysis, reflection, and research.

Activity 4.1: *Checklist for Close Reading*

Learner Objective

To provide a checklist for students to develop the skill of close reading.

Assignment

Students may work alone or with a peer and follow this suggested process on assigned articles/readings:

- Begin by asking students to give the title their attention. What do they expect after reading the title?
- Does the piece have a subtitle? If so, what is the relationship between the title and the subtitle? (By analyzing headlines and subtitles, students can identify the leading ideas.)
- Where is the article placed in the newspaper or magazine? How does its position in the paper or on the page reveal the opinion of the editors?
- What determines the order of the information in the article? What is the lead sentence?
- What is the "hook"?
- Where does a writer place the most important points in the course of the argument?
- What is the logical flow of the argument?

Follow up with more questions from the explanation in chapter 4 for building expert skill in close reading.

Activity 4.2: *The Face-Off*

Learner Objective

The objective of a face-off is to educate and engage, not to find a winner and a loser.

Assignment

The face-off is a debate in its simplest terms. The topic for debate can be selected from the class's ideas about which issues are debatable. This encourages a very active brainstorming session for the entire class. If some suggestions are needed, see the list provided at end of this activity. The issues are listed, and then the argument is framed in the language of a clear, strong statement—and an opposing statement. Students whose turn it is to debate may or may not have the opportunity to choose a particular issue, and they will not know which side of the argument they will be called on to defend, but it is beneficial to build in as many choices and options as is possible so that there is little risk but many possibilities. It works well to ask them their top two issues and then craft an activity, assigning all students one of their top two. Nevertheless, they need to be ready to defend either side of the issue.

Establish the topic in the class before the face-off. Select or sign up four students willing to engage with the issue in two teams of two. Both teams are charged with researching conflicting issues concerning the topic, and they do not know which side they will have to defend. These four are your experts on the topic when they come into class on debate day.

When class convenes, ceremoniously flip a coin to determine which team will defend which side of the issue. Arrange the four chairs, if possible, so that their side of the issue (pro or con) is visible to the audience. The audience should take notes on the arguments presented, not only on the content but also on the quality of the argument and the use of supporting evidence. Prepare hand-outs for students to help structure their note taking during the debate.

The argument begins with one member of each team presenting the basic argument for his or her side (five minutes). The other member of the team is free to add to the points made (three minutes). Then the opposing team, given equal time, adds to the complexity of the argument by presenting points of evidence for their side. The argument may add one more round of debate, a controlled back-and-forth, but the face-off should end with one round of closing arguments.

At this point, the entire discussion is thrown open to the audience, who can ask questions or add ideas. The instructor can add his or her questions to make sure that the entire issue is fully fleshed out.

The activity closes with all members writing their opinion based on the presented evidence. If desired, this reflection could be judged on a provided template that requires that each student defend his or her opinion with specific references to the debate or to the evidence presented.

Students look forward to face-off days, and everyone gets the opportunity to participate. There is not a lot of personal risk for students here, as each person works as a member of a team and prepares points in advance. The activity does, however, allow students to express their opinions, including opinions on the opposite side they had to argue. The educational purpose is to have them understand the issues being researched. The learner outcomes include their consideration of how to understand both sides of an argument before they frame their own side or issue. For further templates and ideas to support this activity, see McGraw-Hill Contemporary Learning at http://www.mhcls.com/usingts/usingts.pdf.

Suggested Topics for Debate

1. All students in high school should have an after-school job.
2. Every student should be required to take a performing arts course.
3. Homework should be banned.
4. School uniforms should be required.
5. Year-round education is not a good idea for student learning.
6. The legal drinking age should be lowered to 18.
7. Physical education should be required of all students throughout high school.
8. All students should be required to perform one year of community service.
9. Schools should block YouTube.
10. All parents should be required to attend parenting classes before having a child.

11. Single-sex schools are better for students.
12. Students should be held legally responsible for bullying in schools.
13. Cyberbullying that occurs outside of school should be punished by the school.
14. Teachers should not be allowed to contact students through social media.
15. High-stakes state testing should be abolished.
16. Should America provide foreign aid to countries that do not allow girls to go to school?
17. It is never appropriate for the government to restrict freedom of speech.
18. Human cloning should be banned.
19. Poetry should be removed from the curriculum.
20. Renewable forms of energy should be subsidized by the government.

Activity Templates

Name: _____

1. What is the issue that is being debated:

2. State the PRO position as the team presented it.

3. What evidence did they use?

4. State the CON position as the team presented it.

5. What evidence did they use?

6. From listening to the debate, indicate THREE main areas of disagreement between the two positions:

    1._____

    2._____

    3. _____

7. Which position (PRO or CON) was stronger and why?

8. Did either position change your viewpoint? How? Explain in your own words.

Name: _____

1. Briefly state in your own words three facts presented by Pro position:

    1._____

    2._____

    3._____

2. Briefly state in your own words three facts presented by Con position:

    1._____

    2._____

    3._____

3. Identify in your own words, evidence that both sides used in their argument:

PRO POSITION:_____

_____

_____

CON POSITION:_____

_____

_____

1. Was there oversimplification in either position? If so, provide evidence.

2. Were there FAULTY generalizations used in either position? If so, provide evidence.

3. Other comments: _____

Summative Assessment

Students write a personal evaluation of the issue, grounding their opinion on evidence derived from their notes.

Universal Design for Learning Application

Engagement (stimulate interest and motivation for learning)—The element of choice provides student engagement, and the student's final reflection is their own opinion.

Representation (present information and content in different ways)—Use template for supported note taking.

Action and expression (differentiate the ways that students can express what they know)—Opinion may be written as a bulleted list, if necessary, with a short opinion statement at the end of the list. Whose argument was stronger?

Activity 4.3: *The Scaffolded Oral Presentation*

Learner Objective

This series of oral arguments helps build students' skills of argumentation while also gradually adding to their confidence.

Assignment

Begin at first by having students locate (or by handing out) a written opinion article to read and present to the class. Students can either write, speak, or visually represent its logic and its value as they see it. This activity could be an early part of a public speaking sequence or may have a written product instead, but in either case it should involve some oral component, such as partnering up to share ideas before the actual oral presentation or writing is required.

In stage 2, the teacher assigns the reading of two articles on the same topic but with opposing points of view. Teachers should assign the articles, ensuring content rigor and access and knowing the reading levels of their students. This task requires students to summarize and analyze each article and then compare articles. However, the student is free to present both articles one at a time or to compare the articles. Allowing students to choose the format for this summary will be motivational. In the summary presentation, the student evaluates the evidence and presents an argument as to which of the two viewpoints is the more compelling.

In stage 3, students argue their own views of an assigned topic. They should find at least three well-supported opinions from reliable sources to integrate into the presentation of their views.

This series of scaffolded assignments helps students develop their confidence, their skill of presentation, and their logic. It gradually increases the number of sources and invites a more sophisticated argument with each additional stage.

Students Who Require Extensive Support

Students who require extensive support will benefit from having a visual to assist them in better organizing and writing their understanding of their comparisons. Something as simple as a color-coded Venn diagram will help organize and guide their thinking.

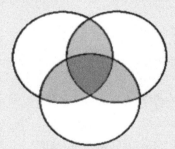

Summative Assessment

For a presentation rubric, use Rubicon (http://www.rubicon.com) or another appropriate rubric website, or, if there is time, have the students design the rubric.

Universal Design for Learning Application

    Engagement (stimulate interest and motivation for learning)—Students may work in
    pairs or small groups to discuss pertinent article facts and features.

    Representation (present information and content in different ways)—Allow students
    to read and discuss their article prior to the whole-class activity.

    *Action and expression (differentiate the ways that students can express what they
    know)*—Students can prepare their written cues with partners before the pre-
    sentation. Students may use any suitable visual supports for their presentation:
    PowerPoints, Prezis, videos, chart paper, and so on.

Activity 4.4: *Panel Discussion*

Learner Objective

Students research the views of a particular person or character to determine opinions,
worldview, or philosophy of that person or character. They must extrapolate from
that information and, to the best of their knowledge, participate in a discussion
with other students in their varying personas. This can be inferential and, at times,
creative. It could be used as a preliminary activity to writing an argument from a
particular point of view.

Assignment

Students take on a persona and research that person's philosophy and views as
preparation for debate. Students enjoy dressing for the occasion. The debate might
be among presidents, candidates, or philosophers or may even be various characters
from books. Depending on the age and ability of the students, have them develop a
profile of their character and determine what that character's views or feelings might
be about life and circumstances.

    For example, there could be a panel discussion with Socrates, Aristotle, the apostle
Paul, and Pericles, who might debate the uses of education, human suffering, or the
perfect man, or with characters in *The Great Gatsby* exchanging views about wealth
or love. Or Thomas Paine, Benjamin Franklin, Sam Adams, King George, and a
loyalist join the panel to discuss the future of America.

    In history class, the class could select a group of figures from a unit on the "Roar-
ing Twenties," such as Al Capone, a flapper, Josephine Baker, and Charlie Chaplin.
In science class, select a group of scientists discussing a vital topic or concern, such as
climate change. This activity can be run as a "fishbowl" (https://www.facinghistory.org/
for-educators/educator-resources/teaching-strategy/fishbowl; https://www.learner
.org/workshops/tml/workshop3/teaching2.html).

    Alternatively, the research can be done collaboratively in teams that create notes
for their character and offer support.

Summative Assessment

Evaluate students' knowledge via a simple teacher rubric: Was the information accurate?

Universal Design for Learning Application

> *Engagement (stimulate interest and motivation for learning)*—The element of choice provides student engagement. Students choose whether to be in the outside circle or inside circle of the fishbowl. Group work as part of the research provides small-group learning experiences.
>
> *Representation (present information and content in different ways)*—Simulation may be recorded for future video use.
>
> *Action and expression (differentiate the ways that students can express what they know)*—Access to all can be provided by having students work in groups to trace a life-size figure on poster paper and "dress" the figure authentically as well as add specific details required by the teacher. Teacher rubric evaluates factual content of simulation.

Activity 4.5: *Staging the Trial*

Learner Objective

As in Activity 4.3, students research their roles in advance, relying on their texts for evidence of their characters' positions and life experiences.

Assignment

This activity offers the opportunity for a different dramatic production that engages, includes, and motivates: the staging of the trial of a literary, scientific, mathematical, or historic character. Students are judge, lawyers, special expert witnesses, the jury, and, of course, the defendant. The evidence is textual, and both sides, ready to research quotations as evidence that may be challenged, retain an expert. Books that lend themselves well are *The Crucible, The Hunger Games, Lord of the Flies*, a new (or old) take on *To Kill a Mockingbird, Crime and Punishment*, and many others. The class could take a case from history, such as the trial of Galileo in science or the Scopes Trial in social studies or science. Another possibility is to draw on current or past newspapers on an issue such as climate change, gun control, or the right to vote. Make sure the topic challenges but also lends itself to include students of all abilities and interests.

Formative Assessment

Students write a final verdict for the trial, briefly explaining their position that the teacher may assess for understanding to determine future instruction.

Universal Design for Learning Application

Engagement (stimulate interest and motivation for learning)—The element of choice provides student engagement, as does the trial enactment.

Representation (present information and content in different ways)—Information is presented via a mock trial, thus providing a wide range of media for understanding.

Action and expression (differentiate the ways that students can express what they know)—Students may use a bulleted list to explain their position or fill in a teacher-made template. My verdict is _____ because _____.

Activity 4.6: *Defending Preference*

Learner Objective

Students research multiple approaches in order to choose and then defend the choice of which two are most useful or compelling. The argument is written.

Assignment

The student finds five opinions or perspectives on the same subject. After summarizing each in a paragraph, laying out the authors' individual perspectives, the student chooses two that seem the most helpful to understanding the issue. The student then argues why those two are most compelling or convincing. This exercise can be done with any middle or secondary grade, choosing reading at the appropriate level. Multiple newspaper reports, editorials, movie reviews, or other such materials will work for this activity. Political cartoons could be used effectively.

For high-performing readers, we can raise the bar and have them research five different critical views of a novel they have read in their high school careers. The critical schools might represent views like formalism, Freudian criticism, feminist criticism, reader response, biographical or historical, and so on. Then the student argues for two that he or she feels are most useful in understanding that particular novel. This is a good introduction to literary schools of criticism as well as argument. The critical texts provide points of evidence the student may cite.

For students who like to draw or for those who like to work with computers, this activity provides a great opportunity to visualize their five or more sources through computer programs or sketches or whatever other media that they could suggest as well as what the teacher offers.

In this activity, the preference of each student is not judged. Rather, the logical defense of their preference, using evidence found in text, is the objective. A template is useful to aid students in organizing their material.

Activity 4.6. *Defending Your Preference*

Sources Used (Opinions or Perspectives):

1.	2.	3.	4.	5.

Summarize each source on a separate page. Then have students draft their response for their argument on their two best sources.

Formative Assessment

Check on the suitability of the five options before continuing. Use the above template for a formative assessment opportunity.

Summative Assessment

Written evaluation of the final paper. Why are the two views you chose most useful in comprehending the issue?

Universal Design for Learning Application

Engagement (stimulate interest and motivation for learning)—The choice of media types or genres facilitates student engagement.

Representation (present information and content in different ways)—Teachers may reduce the number of viewpoints from five to a lesser number.

Action and expression (differentiate the ways that students can express what they know)—Students may show their understanding through a variety of media: captioned videos, PowerPoints, Prezis, posters, and so on.

5

Learning to Write by Reading Poetry

Don't tell me the moon is shining; show me the glint of light on broken glass.

—Anton Chekhov

A well-constructed poem is not so different from an essay: both are economical, both are purposeful though they engage us differently, and both attempt to evoke a response from the reader by skillfully arranging their carefully chosen words, images, and details into a syntactical design. This book does not purport to teach poetry writing; rather, it will explore how reading and writing poetry can contribute to our becoming masterful writers.

Poetry is an arrangement of words that concentrates both feeling and meaning. It is writing intensified. Its elements are most deliberately selected. In other words, good poetry is good writing taken to the limit.

A reader may well question, The limit of what? Sometimes, the poet pushes the limits of understanding—and then it's only natural to push back! How many students by high school admit to enjoying poetry? (See Activity 5.1: *Less Is More*.)

HOW TO READ A POEM

A poem is a carefully wrapped present, a gift waiting to be opened. If students learn to anticipate the pleasure, delayed until opened and enjoyed, they will fare better. Teach them to unwrap it slowly and carefully in order to see what they have. Make poetry reading a low-risk activity, accepting all honest responses as valid ones. By maintaining an attitude of discovery, students may enjoy the poem and the pursuit of capturing its essence.

Sometimes, returning to a poem in another week or month will finally cap the pleasure of reading. Students love what has become familiar, even if they may object to rereading. If the teacher can get students to associate the challenge of a poem with pleasure, not pain, poetry will have a convert. What can teachers do to motivate students to read and reflect on poetry? Authentic poetry written by peers or poetry that reflects authentic experiences may help engage students. (See Activity 5.2: *"Found" Poetry*.)

THE POWER OF POETRY

When readers read poetry, they consider the choices a poet made to craft it. When writers write poetry, they consider the reader's response. Teachers hope students will recognize the value of both perspectives. To be a poet or a lover of poetry requires most of the same skills. What, then, can poetry teach us?

First, poetry is intense. It is economical. Fewer words can result in more potent constructions and sparer expressions. In poetry, each word has more weight. Nothing is wasted. This does not mean, however, that the selected words must be fancy, heavy, or anything else. They just have to be the right words for the purpose. *Read Write Think* offers interactive planners to scaffold students' writing of diamante poetry (http://www.readwritethink.org/classroom-resources/student-interactives/diamante-poems-30053.html) and acrostic poetry (http://www.readwritethink.org/classroom-resources/student-interactives/acrostic-poems-30045.html). (See Activity 5.3: *From Prose to Poetry*.)

Sound can be both surprising and entertaining. Shouldn't prose also appeal to the ear as well as the eye? Poetic prose will stimulate both the mind and emotion through skillful employment of sound, just as much as poetry, though it is less likely to be noticed. Consider, for example, the value of onomatopoeia, which we consider a "poetic device" but which is actually at work in everything we say and everything we write because English is replete with words that sound like what they mean. Why not use it deliberately in prose as well as poetry? Why not teach onomatopoeia using sports poetry and then have students incorporate it into their writing? (http://www.readwritethink.org/classroom-resources/lesson-plans/swish-whack-teaching-onomatopoeia-1131.html). When the writer wants to provoke engagement at a more visceral level, why not employ sound? Embrace alliteration for effect—but never subvert your purpose. Be subtle but wield control of all the elements.

A writer may arrange the page to please the eye. White space can be used for effect. Karen Hesse's *Out of the Dust* (1997) and Pamela Porter's *The Crazy Man* (2005), both novels written for young adults, accomplish this admirably. Even without rhyme or meter, the pages come across to the reader as poetic, and the effect is that they appear to express an emotional truth, like poetry.

A good writer may use patterns to build expectations on the part of the reader. Repetition of a word or phrase can do this. Starting several sentences the same way can also do it. Rhetorical speech has long been used to please the ear and so is effective, though it may be too heavy-handed or obvious on the written page. Threading a key word or phrase into every paragraph gradually creates an echo that resonates in the unconscious mind of the reader, reinforcing impact and constructing meaning.

Students can experiment with syntax. Poetry will challenge one's understanding of grammar, but it will also help one understand the rules, the flexibility of the language, and the bounds of syntax for different purposes. The dance of the sentence in prose does not necessarily align with the dance of the sentence in poetry. Where are the boundaries? Meaning and sense are the ultimate arbiters. Use poetry to help students break out of the straitjacket.

Syntax should be constructed to make the most of patterning. A good writer may begin with long sentences but then interject a short sentence to break the train of thought. Long sentences can help build tension, but a short sentence suddenly makes the reader realize she has been holding her breath! Good writing is straightforward in expression: subject–verb–object. Then, at the opportune moment, the order may shift. This might seem like a difficult thing to do—unless one is a reader of poetry. Surprise your reader by dashing expectation! Play with words. Repeat a word or phrase deliberately, for effect, but be subtle. Do not annoy your reader unless that is the reaction you are seeking!

Prose has rhythms, just not meter. Pay attention to the rhythms of prose. Poetry can teach us how. We read a lot of prose every day that is in iambic pentameter, but we don't notice. There is a reason that so much of our traditional poetry is in iambic pentameter: That is the default rhythm of the language! In tetrameter (four beats to a line), lines move quickly. Pentameter (five beats to a line) has some gravity, maintaining a line long enough to support more complex ideas. It's easy to find that rhythm in an ordinary sentence. What a wonderful opportunity to connect with music educators. Show a short YouTube video to introduce or reinforce this concept (http://www.youtube.com/watch?v=Ec_pDV07pQg). (See Activity 5.4: *Playing with Meter* and Activity 5.5: *Learning from e.e. cummings.*)

We can use sensory detail/imagery. When we appeal to the senses, we feel alive!

Metaphor is the natural shortcut to vicarious experience. Metaphor makes it unnecessary to do or say "it all." No one can possibly do it all anyway. Take a shortcut with a well-constructed metaphor: I don't ski. How can I know what it feels like to fly down that hill on skis? Metaphor! Compare it to something else in my experience.

Most figures of speech are simply a form of metaphor. Consider simile, personification, oxymoron, metonymy, synecdoche, or symbol. All are modes of comparison, or varieties of metaphor. It is how the human brain learns best! What is it like? We build webs of knowledge through actual experience *and* representative experience. Language helps us build bridges in our brains from one to the other. Metaphor can often do what description cannot accomplish. (See Activity 5.6: *Poems Using Metaphor.*)

The first objective in working with poetry is helping students recognize figures of speech (metaphoric language) and how they contribute to meaning in a poem—or wherever they read it. Learning to label various types of metaphoric language should be of secondary importance, especially in the lower grades and with less skillful readers. The first order of business is understanding and enjoyment.

ENCOURAGING ALL STUDENTS

A cautionary note about writing poetry: So many students are discouraged because they have been criticized in their reading and writing of poetry. But how many high school teachers are in a position to judge the budding poet? The same might be said of the budding artist. Many have taken art classes in school, which convinced them that they had no talent, yet later in life they find that they are able enough to create products that are of interest to many!

Art, whether verbal or pictorial, is healthy and exciting, at least to the artist. Let's withhold judgment in such cases and encourage everyone to express themselves in artistic ways. Too many students graduate with a negative idea of their creative abilities. Like literacy, creativity is a lifelong endeavor. It is wrong to discourage the creative effort, no matter the judgment concerning the immediate product. (See Activity 5.7: *Letter Poem*.)

POETRY ABOUT THE REAL WORLD

There is much good poetry that is not abstract and that is accessible to all students, including those who may be disengaged. The following books have well-written "nonfiction poems" encompassing a wide variety of formats:

- *Night of the Republic* by Alan Shapiro (2012)—night tour of America's public places (a gas station restroom, shoe store, and so on)
- *Joyful Noise, Poems for Two Voices* by Paul Fleishman (1988)—this Newbery Award book offers poetry on insects
- *Once upon Ice* by Jane Yolen (2003)—offers poems about winter
- *Wild Wings* (2002) and *An Egret's Day* (2010) by Jane Yolen—offer nonfiction poems that could be enjoyed by students achieving well below grade level

A number of nonfiction historical poems could be used to introduce a unit of study or be part of a unit of study. They can be current poems, such as "Still I Rise" by Maya Angelou (http://www.poets.org/poetsorg/poem/still-i-rise), or traditional historical poems, such as "Paul Revere's Ride" by Henry Wadsworth Longfellow (http://www.poets.org/poetsorg/poem/paul-reveres-ride). Poetry links the content with the voice of the poet and creates images for many students that they would not get from a textbook. "Freedom's Plow" by Langston Hughes (http://www.poemhunter.com/poem/freedom-s-plow) can be used to introduce sharecropping in the South, or

"Lines on the Loss of the Titanic" by Thomas Hardy (http://www.poetryfoundation .org/poem/176678) can emphasize the impact of such a loss of human lives and can be juxtaposed with a modern poem on the impact of 9/11.

There are poems on states, holidays, patriotism and certain patriots, immigration, wars, protest, and myriad topics and events. There are so many poems that could be integrated into the content, especially in social studies, to provide thoughtful, multiple perspectives on a period or an era in history. (See Activity 5.8: *History and Poetry*.)

MORE REASONS TO EMBRACE POETRY

Students love music but often fail to recognize the musicality of their own language. Finding music and writing song lyrics is motivating and entertaining while it reinforces the elements of poetry. Rhythm, rhyme, imagery—poetry has it all, and so can well-written prose. (See Activity 5.9: *Songs as Poetry*.)

Students can be discouraged when they cannot grasp the underlying message and nuance of a poem. They need to be patient and learn to love a mystery or a puzzle. Teachers need to be patient with students, being mindful that judgment may kill students' enjoyment. It is okay to be temporarily clueless. Next week, revisit the poem and see if it speaks. Or next month or in the spring. Recognize what is missing or implied for more study. Inference is difficult but worthwhile. (See Activity 5.10: *Inference*, which distinguishes what is said from what is not said in a poem.)

By reading and writing poetry, students "tune up" their skills to prepare them to write powerful, even entertaining, prose. Poetry books written by adolescents and young adults may also aid in engaging disengaged students with poetry:

- *Believe Me I Know* (Valerie Chow Bush, editor, 2002) offers poems by young people who have not lived easy lives.
- *I Am the Darker Brother: An Anthology of Modern Poems by African Americans* (Arnold Adoff and Benny Andrews, editors, 1968) provides a poem for every occasion, whether happy, sad, excited, morbid, nature oriented, and so on.
- *Time You Let Me In: 25 Poets under 25* (Naomi Shihab Nye, editor, 2010) is a lively collection of poems by young contemporary writers: poems for teens by teens.

Many of these sources may be used for the activities mentioned in this chapter. Poetry should be accessible to all—both in the reading and in the writing. It is to hand over control of language to our students—to allow the bird to fly. May all budding writers of both poetry and prose experience the pleasure and creative excitement of reading and writing poetically.

ACTIVITIES FOR CHAPTER 5

These activities address the Common Core Standards for reading and writing, providing teachers with a shared vision of literacy across the disciplines. The following standards in both reading and writing govern the suggested strategies that follow.

Target Anchor Standards for Reading

Standard 1. Read closely to determine what the text says explicitly and to make logical inferences from it; cite specific textual evidence when writing or speaking to support conclusions drawn from the text.

Standard 4. Interpret words and phrases as they are used in a text, including determining technical, connotative, and figurative meanings, and analyze how specific word choices shape meaning and tone.

Target Anchor Standards in Writing

Standard 4. Produce clear and coherent writing in which the development, organization, and style are appropriate to task, purpose, and audience.

Activity 5.1: *Less Is More*

Learner Objective

Students will cut unnecessary words from writing. This activity teaches students to be economical in their writing.

Assignment

Students should randomly choose a sample of past writing. Students should be directed to rewrite the piece using half as many words. Have them justify their editing choices. Ensure that they preserve the original meaning. They will soon discover that most all the pieces they have written would benefit by being more terse. Fewer words can pack more power.

Formative Assessment

Teachers review students' edited page and rationale for changes to determine understanding of economical writing. Does the product still have all the information it needs? Is the piece still fluent?

Universal Design for Learning Application

Engagement (stimulate interest and motivation for learning)—Students will be motivated by choosing a previous work sample for this activity.

Representation (present information and content in different ways)—Students may benefit from using a computer program for this activity. Others may find it easier to do this as a pencil-and-paper task.

Action and expression (differentiate the ways that students can express what they know)—Allow students to demonstrate their understanding through peer readings of "before and after" work while counting the words.

Activity 5.2: "Found" Poetry

Learner Objective

Students select words from prose that they arrange to create a poem. This activity teaches students to develop an "eye" for the right word. Students will transfer this skill to improve their own word choices in their written work.

Assignment

An extension of Activity 5.1 is developed in found poetry—that is, poetry designed by the student reader from words taken directly from a short piece, page, article, or other work. The assignment might be to write a poem of fewer than 30 words, all taken from one piece, page, article, and so on. The students must choose (or cut and paste) words that will capture the intent in a more abstract and intense way. They must learn to read between the lines to construct meaning. In a found poem, they have to construct the full meaning with a few deft strokes. This raises "diction" to a new plane.

Creating a "found" poem can be done as follows:

- Select a text of modest length or select a page or passage that can showcase an idea or point of view. This might be a news article, or it could be a passage from a book or play. Have students mark or highlight the text, identifying the most powerful, interesting, or distinctive words and phrases in the original text.
- Identify the main idea so that the found poem reflects the meaning intended. (Upper grades may decide to create a poem that is a parody or a satire on the original, but this is difficult to do well. Some will love the challenge!)
- Arrange selected words on the page, maximizing the use of the white space available. Allow some flexibility with sentence structure but don't sacrifice logic or effect on the reader.
- Students will want to make it rhyme and may sacrifice to get it. Let them experiment, if they insist, but they must work only with the author's actual words.

Point out the opportunities to incorporate rhythm, repetition, alliteration, or metaphor. Celebrate students' successful incorporation of any poetic devices.
- Require a draft process, ending on a final, perfect presentation of the words.
- Optional: Have them illustrate their poems and display them, next to the prose that inspired them.

Here, the authors model the technique, using a short speech delivered by Sojourner Truth, a former slave, speaking to the Women's Convention in Akron, Ohio, in 1851. Provide students with the text and have them find in its words the words of the author-created poem, highlighting the words as they find them in the speech. They can then take the same speech (or another text to work with) and "find" their own poems.

Sojourner Truth (1797–1883): Ain't I a Woman?

Well, children, where there is so much racket there must be something out of kilter. I think that 'twixt the negroes of the South and the women at the North, all talking about rights, the white men will be in a fix pretty soon. But what's all this here talking about?

That man over there says that women need to be helped into carriages, and lifted over ditches, and to have the best place everywhere. Nobody ever helps me into carriages, or over mud-puddles, or gives me any best place! And ain't I a woman? Look at me! Look at my arm! I have ploughed and planted, and gathered into barns, and no man could head me! And ain't I a woman? I could work as much and eat as much as a man—when I could get it—and bear the lash as well! And ain't I a woman? I have borne thirteen children, and seen most all sold off to slavery, and when I cried out with my mother's grief, none but Jesus heard me! And ain't I a woman?

Then they talk about this thing in the head; what's this they call it? [member of audience whispers, "intellect"] That's it, honey. What's that got to do with women's rights or negroes' rights? If my cup won't hold but a pint, and yours holds a quart, wouldn't you be mean not to let me have my little half measure full?

Then that little man in black there, he says women can't have as much rights as men, 'cause Christ wasn't a woman! Where did your Christ come from? Where did your Christ come from? From God and a woman! Man had nothing to do with Him.

If the first woman God ever made was strong enough to turn the world upside down all alone, these women together ought to be able to turn it back , and get it right side up again! And now they is asking to do it, the men better let them.

Obliged to you for hearing me, and now old Sojourner ain't got nothing more to say.

Following is the authors' found poem based on *Ain't I a Woman* by Sojourner Truth:

Something out of kilter—
    But what's all this here talking about?
Look at this arm! I ploughed and planted
 and gathered into barns,
I work as much and eat as much as a man—
when I can get it,

and bear the lash as well,
    Ain't I a woman?
When I, a slave, cried out with mother's grief,
    none but Jesus heard me.
Nobody ever helps me.
And ain't I a woman?
Christ came from God and woman
    not from a man.
Women ought to turn it back
and get it right side up again!

Formative Assessment

Teacher reviews first draft of the found poem to determine if the student captured the essence of the article and made it more intense in poetic form.

Universal Design for Learning Application

Engagement (stimulate interest and motivation for learning)—Students may choose their text.

Representation (present information and content in different ways)—Students may highlight using a computer program or by hand.

Action and expression (differentiate the ways that students can express what they know)—Allow students to show their understanding by sharing their poem with peers visually, orally, or through video.

Activity 5.3: *From Prose to Poetry*

Learner Objective

Students compare word arrangements in prose and also in poetry. This activity asks students to consider the effect of one arrangement or another.

Assignment

Select (or have students select) a paragraph or two from a book or article or from student writing. It should have an idea expressed or the development of a thought or action. It would be especially good if the passage ends with a surprise or a shift of emotion.

Students rearrange the entire piece into verse form, utilizing the white space to create a visual effect, breaking strings of words and placing them in a creative order as a poem. Have students share the result and explain how a writer can manipulate how a reader reads and understands a written piece. Display the prose next to the poem so that the effect can be enjoyed. Jon Anderson's poem "The Parachutist" is an excellent example of this prose-to-poetry transformation. As the parachutist drifts through the air (and the page) and people on the ground watch him fall, it finally becomes clear to all that he will meet water, not land, when he reaches Earth.

A single paragraph from Edgar Allan Poe's "The Tell-Tale Heart" illustrates the process:

> TRUE! — nervous — very, very dreadfully nervous I had been and am; but why will you say that I am mad? The disease had sharpened my senses — not destroyed — not dulled them. Above all was the sense of hearing acute. I heard all things in the heaven and in the earth. I heard many things in hell. How, then, am I mad? Hearken! and observe how healthily — how calmly I can tell you the whole story.

Here is a model of the process in a "poem" created by the authors of a single paragraph from "The Tell-Tale Heart" by Edgar Allan Poe:

TRUE!
---- nervous ---- very, very dreadfully nervous
I had been and am; but
Why will you say I am mad?
The disease
had sharpened my senses ---
                    not destroyed –
                    not dulled them. Above all was the sense
                    of hearing acute.
        I heard all things in the heaven and in the earth.
        I heard many things in hell.
How, then, am I mad?
Hearken!
And observe how healthily
        how calmly I can tell you
                    the
                            whole
                                story.

Formative Assessment

Teachers determine if students understand how word arrangement can affect the emotional response of the reader. This activity determines if students are now ready to use this poem as a model for translating a prose passage into poetry.

Universal Design for Learning Application

Engagement (stimulate interest and motivation for learning)—Allow students to work in small groups.

Representation (present information and content in different ways)—Students may experiment with orally reading the two selections.

Action and expression (differentiate the ways that students can express what they know)—Students discuss the differences noted by the oral readings. A poem may suggest an illustration for students to draw or represent via a computer program. A poster could be developed for the poem using multiple illustrations.

Activity 5.4: *Playing with Meter*

Learner Objective

Students practice speaking and writing in a meter. This activity promotes effective writing by increasing sensitivity to rhythm in language. Good writing incorporates the rhythm of language. Students can read prose and identify rhythmic lines.

Assignment

A fun activity in class is to challenge the class to say whatever they say in iambic pentameter (blank verse). Iambic pentameter is the natural rhythm of the English sentence. Once you establish the rhythm, they will hear it. Tell them that for half an hour, they have to converse in iambic pentameter.

A beginning could be as follows:

If you can make a game of it one time/
You will no doubt have trouble in the end,/
For you and all your students, like as not,/
Will ne'er continue your old ways again./
You will hear rhythm ev'rywhere you go/
As this, my playful exercise will show!

Have students follow up by writing a letter in iambic pentameter to a friend. If they wish, they can add rhyme to create couplets. You will turn your students into Shakespeare "wannabes," possibly rhyming fools.

Formative Assessment

Teacher reviews letters to determine if students understand rhythm in language. Teachers may also ask students to find words out of a word list that are iambic, such as *inform*, *detract*, and *expel*, or phrases, such as *in fact*, *of course*, and *we will*. Do students understand iambic pentameter as demonstrated in their letter, or is more instruction needed?

Universal Design for Learning Application

Engagement (stimulate interest and motivation for learning)—Have students work in partners. Beat out rhythms physically tapping the desk.

Representation (present information and content in different ways)—Provide a variety of examples for students. Begin with a very simple meter, such as "Mary Had a Little Lamb" or "Twinkle, Twinkle, Little Star." Model using a simple poem's meter to guide writing a new poem using words provided from the class as a whole.

Action and expression (differentiate the ways that students can express what they know)—Allow students to demonstrate their understanding through writing by producing PowerPoints, Prezis, or videos or producing a project-based demonstration of knowledge—possibly a visual poster representation of their model poem and then their original rewriting of their own poem using their own words.

Activity 5.5: *Learning from e.e. cummings*

Learner Objective

This activity allows students to experiment with language. Poetry permits more flexibility than prose. Students' experimentations expand their range of writing techniques, which in many cases can be transferred to other writing activities. Students learn that words are fun and that, at least once in a while, it's okay to break rules if one has a reason. Students practice applying terms such as *alliteration* and *metaphor* in their class conversations, thus increasing understanding.

Assignment

In this activity, students experiment with language for effect by imitating e.e. cummings.

Let's read two poems by e.e. cummings and see what we can learn about good writing and keeping (or breaking) the rules:

- *Maggie and Molly* and *Milly and May*—poem read on YouTube (http://www .youtube.com/watch?v=PZ_06r0OGR4)
- *Maggie and Molly* and *Milly and May* (http://writersalmanac.publicradio.org/ index.php?date=2002/03/07)

Cummings takes his usual poetic license. He takes us back to our childhood, but the result is not childish. He makes a conclusion that is both charming and thoughtful:

- *--Just Spring*—e.e. cummings reads *Just Spring* on YouTube (http://www .youtube.com/watch?v=NA836Ax7scw, http://www.poetryfoundation.org/ poem/176657)

Analyze for alliteration, rhythm (playful and energetic), sensory detail, metaphor (in the broader sense), sound (rhyme, alliteration, and so on), surprise (especially breaks in the rhyme and rhythm that get our attention and signal adventure), and things that are not always harmonious. Which rules of writing does e.e. cummings discard and why?

Formative Assessment

This is a modeling activity guided by the teacher. The teacher simply observes student comments for understanding language flexibility. When do you need rules, and when don't you need rules? Monitor students' use of alliteration, rhythm, sensory detail, metaphor, and rhyme to guide future instruction.

Universal Design for Learning Application

Engagement (stimulate interest and motivation for learning)—Have students choose a partner for this activity.

Representation (present information and content in different ways)—Use YouTube websites to garner interest in e.e. cummings.

Action and expression (differentiate the ways that students can express what they know)—Allow students to demonstrate their understanding through writing by producing PowerPoints or Prezis or producing a project-based demonstration of knowledge—possibly a visual poster representation of their understanding.

Activity 5.6: *Poems Using Metaphor*

Learner Objective

Students identify and explain metaphoric language. This activity is a precursor to students using metaphoric language in their own writing. Students should hear as well as see the poem.

Assignment

The teacher models the reading of the poetry for student understanding. Then the students read the poem aloud with a partner and find and discuss the metaphoric language. This is a wonderful paired activity.

For Students Who Require Extensive Support

Jane Yolen's poetry collections offer numerous examples of nonfiction poetry easily accessible to all students. See References for book titles.

Identify the metaphoric language in three classic poems. Look for other poems for students that have powerful central metaphors. In each of the poems, have students explain how comparison creates images in the reader's mind.

The Eagle by Alfred Lord Tennyson
He clasps the crag with crooked hands;
Close to the sun in lonely lands,
Ring'd with the azure world, he stands.
The wrinkled sea beneath him crawls;
He watches from his mountain walls,
And like a thunderbolt he falls.

Daffodils by William Wordsworth
I wandered lonely as a cloud
That floats on high o'er vales and hills,
When all at once I saw a crowd,
A host, of golden daffodils;
Beside the lake, beneath the trees,
Fluttering and dancing in the breeze.

Continuous as the stars that shine
And twinkle on the milky way,
They stretched in never-ending line
Along the margin of a bay:
Ten thousand saw I at a glance,
Tossing their heads in sprightly dance.

The waves beside them danced; but they
Out-did the sparkling waves in glee:
A poet could not but be gay,
In such a jocund company:
I gazed—and gazed—but little thought
What wealth the show to me had brought:

For oft, when on my couch I lie
In vacant or in pensive mood,
They flash upon that inward eye
Which is the bliss of solitude;
And then my heart with pleasure fills,
And dances with the daffodils.

Meditation XVII by John Donne
No man is an island,
Entire of itself,
Every man is a piece of the continent,
A part of the main.
If a clod be washed away by the sea,

Europe is the less.
As well as if a promontory were.
As well as if a manor of thy friend's
Or of thine own were:
Any man's death diminishes me,
Because I am involved in mankind,
And therefore never send to know for whom the bell tolls;
It tolls for thee.

Students Who Require Extensive Support

Students who require extensive support will have difficulty identifying truth/reality from fantasy both in literature as well as in their own lives. Teachers will have to provide numerous examples and have students "practice" identifying truth from fantasy. Using stories the students are already very familiar with in conjunction with corresponding pictures and photographs will assist students in acquiring the ability to identify the differences. These students will experience maximum success if students use pictures from well-known stories for fantasy. When possible, use photographs with the student him- or herself in it. These pages should become part of the student's language arts notebook.

Fantasy/Pretend	Truth/Reality
Use clip-art picture here	*Use photograph here*

Formative Assessment

Students in each group will identify and explain metaphoric images to the class. Are students ready to move on, or is more instruction needed in this area?

Universal Design for Learning Application

Engagement (stimulate interest and motivation for learning)—Allow students to choose a partner for this activity.

Representation (present information and content in different ways)—Provide students a list of poetry to choose from. Include contemporary works, such as popular music lyrics.

Action and expression (differentiate the ways that students can express what they know)—Allow students to demonstrate their understanding through writing, illustrations, computer-generated work, or drawings using a two-column chart to indicate metaphoric language and its meaning. Capture the feeling that the poem evokes.

Activity 5.7: *Letter Poem*

Learner Objective

Students will create a poem based on borrowed design. This activity inspires students to express their feelings in a letter poem. Students learn through imitating the structure of a model poem to elevate their own writing.

Assignment

Students will write a letter to a person to tell him or her something that has not previously been said. Poet Peter Meinke's "Untitled" poem begins, "This is a poem to my son Peter . . ." and can provide a basic template for the message. Meinke continues with identifying description, "who . . . ," to describe his son and their relationship, continuing to the transitional word "because . . ." to the reason for the letter. He rhymes randomly within the poem but does not allow rhyme to interfere with his message for his son. It expresses his true feelings, letting Peter know what otherwise would remain unexpressed.

Using this bare-bones structure, "This is a poem to _____," and limiting the length of the poem to a page, students create poems that are worthy of a second or third draft. Students write to friends they haven't seen since they were a child. They write to parents or grandparents who have died. They write love letters. They sometimes wrap up their poems for a Christmas gift for the person to whom their poem is addressed.

The following is a sample poem (by a teacher, writing with her students):

This is a poem to my life's friend, Eileen,
Whom I have not seen in thirty years,
Who, when we first met, told me she was twelve,
And when I confessed that I was only nine,
Assured me I could still be her friend.
She attended Catholic school, while I attended public school.
But every day when school was done, we found each other
to play games like Pay Day and Clue and Life.
We played, tennis, baseball, and basketball
And told each other stories in the dark spaces of her attic.
I want to see you again, to always be my friend,
Because you are a part of who I am today, even now.

Formative Assessment

Volunteers will read their poems aloud to the class. All students will be allowed to take their poems home to create a final draft. The final draft may be evaluated by the teacher using whatever criteria makes sense for this particular class of students.

Universal Design for Learning Application

Engagement (stimulate interest and motivation for learning)—Allow students to work with a partner for this activity.

Representation (present information and content in different ways)—Allow students to listen to this poem on tape and have a small-group discussion about the meaning of the poem prior to the whole-class activity.

Action and expression (differentiate the ways that students can express what they know)—Allow students to demonstrate their understanding through writing by producing PowerPoints or Prezis or producing a project-based demonstration of knowledge—possibly a visual poster representation of their understanding.

Activity 5.8: *History and Poetry*

Learner Objective

Students write a historical poem using ideas from a website. This gives students the opportunity to experiment with narrative poetry. Writers must choose their diction, arrange their words, and communicate information about a historical event. This activity engages students in historical material while putting it into poetic form.

Assignment

To add to the use of poetry in a lesson or a unit of study, why not have the students write a historical poem following the directions on PBS History detectives site: http://www.pbs.org/opb/historydetectives/educators/technique-guide/writing-an-historical-poem.

Use a classic poem, such as Lanier's *Battle of Lexington*, or a modern poet's interpretation of the Revolution. The link for the Battle of Lexington is http://www.poetry-archive.com/l/the_battle_of_lexington.html

Why not use Walt Whitman's poem "Oh Captain, My Captain" (http://www.poetryfoundation.org/poem/174742) on Lincoln and the Civil War period as a lead-in to the study of the Civil War? Compare it with other war poems and/or leadership during a specific war.

Read a poem such as Langston Hughes's "A Dream Deferred" (http://www.poetryfoundation.org/poem/175884) and integrate it into the U.S. history class as a viable statement on African American history in the United States. This is an excellent way to use poetry in a social studies/English language arts class.

Students Who Require Extensive Support

Make a bulletin board from the following link—*There Once was a Poem That Knew Facts: The Unlikely Love Affair between Poetry and Nonfiction* (http://www.allanwolf.com/docs/Poetry%20Meets%20NonFiction.pdf)—presented by Allan Wolf. This offers students a valuable reference to use for understanding the "vocabulary" of poetry as well as its numerous formats. This may also be made into laminated pages to insert into the students' language arts notebook to use as a reference.

Formative Assessment

Teachers identify student understanding of a historical event. Teachers review the poem for historical accuracy. Students write a final draft of the poem at home and turn it in to be evaluated by the teacher. The teacher determines if more practice is needed with this activity. Class or individual portfolios may be developed.

Universal Design for Learning Application

Engagement (stimulate interest and motivation for learning)—Students may be paired for this activity.

Representation (present information and content in different ways)—Teacher models activity for the entire class first.

Action and expression (differentiate the ways that students can express what they know)—Allow students to demonstrate their understanding through writing their poem by producing PowerPoints or Prezis or a project-based demonstration of knowledge—possibly a visual poster representation of their understanding.

Activity 5.9: *Songs as Poetry*

Learner Objective

Students use music *without words* to write their own poem songs. This engaging activity increases students' understanding of how music and lyrics go together. Writing the lyrics gives students more practice in word selection, rhythm, and rhyme that transfers to other forms of writing. It provides a structure in which language must fit, similar to a sonnet.

Assignment

Taking "The Star-Spangled Banner," the national anthem, which is truly a poem made into a song, could be great fun, and after dissecting it and what it stands for, have the students write a modern version of the anthem that could still be sung at baseball games! (http://www.scoutsongs.com/lyrics/starspangledbanner.html).

More ideas for incorporating music into lyrics and poetry are the following:

- Have students bring in two hip-hop songs (with no profanity or inappropriate content) to share with the class. Is hip-hop poetry? Have students work in groups to write and record a hip-hop poem. Each group should design a case for their poem and receive individual CDs of their work.
- Continue to examine metaphor through analyzing popular music at this website: http://www.readwritethink.org/classroom-resources/lesson-plans/stairway-heaven-examining-metaphor-975.html.

Formative Assessment

Have students develop their own rubric to use for each activity. This provides students with their own criteria for producing a successful product. Thus, creativity is encouraged, not stymied. Teachers evaluate the final product with the students' rubric. Rubric should include effort. Students may want to develop a marketing plan for their song using persuasive writing.

Universal Design for Learning Application

Engagement (stimulate interest and motivation for learning)—Allow students to choose the music they would like to use for this activity. Caution: Have students choose music that does not have words in the recording (an instrumental selection) when they choose their music. This allows students more creativity when coming up with their own words.

Representation (present information and content in different ways)—Music can be classical, rap, jazz, hip-hop, and so on.

Action and expression (differentiate the ways that students can express what they know)—Students may develop rap music, a dance routine, or visual art to go along with their song.

Activity 5:10: *Inference*

Learner Objective

Students read a poem and analyze what is said in addition to what they must infer.

Assignment

This is a guided practice activity. Teachers may model what is expected from students using the below format. Students then use a two-column chart or other means to identify what is and what is not said in a poem. Students will eventually learn how to use imagery in their own writing.

Find and print out copies of Robert Frost's poem "Nothing Gold Can Stay." In a classroom setting, color coding could be used for this activity. What is directly said in the poem could be in one color (here bolded) and then questions to guide students to infer the poem's meaning in italicized text. Students could use a second color, further accentuating and clarifying this procedure.

Line 1	**In spring, new growth is yellow before green.**
	How can it be green and gold at the same time? Is this about the seasons?
Line 2	**The yellow doesn't stay for long.**
	What does gold mean? Why is it the hardest hue to hold?
Line 3	**Flowers come before leaves.**
	How can a leaf also be a flower?
Line 4	**Flowers briefly bloom and fall off the plant.**
	Is this really an hour? 60 minutes?
Line 5	**Leaves come out.**
	What does "subsides" mean? How do leaves subside?
Line 6	**The Garden of Eden didn't last long**
	What does Eden have to do with this?
Line 7	**Dawn turns into day.**
	How are Eden and dawn alike?
Line 8	**Nothing gold can stay.**
	What is it that's gold? What can't stay?

For Students Who Require Extensive Support

Inference is challenging for many 'at risk' students. One way to teach 'reading between the lines' is to use comic strips (Constable, Grossie, Moniz, & Ryan, 2013) and have students infer what is going on visually. Once students understand that 'inference' refers to understanding text without the words being directly stated, they can practice inferring with short written passages that are provided for them, eventually generalizing these inferences to other more complex texts and their own writing.

INFERENCING WITH WORDS

Bill looked out the window and saw Mom and Dad working in the yard. Dad was mowing the lawn and Mom was planting flowers. Bill heard a very loud noise. Mom and Dad ran in the house. Both Mom and Dad were wet. What happened? Why were Mom and Dad wet?

During the California Gold Rush of 1849, the world's supply of gold more than doubled, and hundreds of thousands of people rushed to California to find their share. Boomtowns popped up to accommodate the visitors. A boomtown is a community that receives sudden and explosive growth and development. San Francisco had around two hundred residents in 1846, and about 36,000 in 1852. The few merchants in these boomtowns sold goods for more than ten times what they cost back East. For example, a single pound of flour sold for as much as $17. Not everyone who joined in the California Gold Rush got rich, but most of the boomtown merchants did.

Why were boomtown merchants able to sell their products for so much money? http://www.ereadingworksheets.com/free-reading-worksheets/reading -comprehension-worksheets/inferences-worksheets/

Formative Assessment

Teachers observe student responses to modeling activity and then proceed to other poems for further practice.

Universal Design for Learning Application

Engagement (stimulate interest and motivation for learning)—Allow students to choose the poem they would like to read from a list provided by the teacher.

Representation (present information and content in different ways)—Use color coding to differentiate what is directly stated in the poem versus what is inferred.

Action and expression (differentiate the ways that students can express what they know)—Allow students to demonstrate their understanding using visual representations of this understanding: pictures, clip art, drawings and so on.

6

Providing Literacy Access to All Students

Reading should not be presented to children as a chore or duty. It should be offered to them as a precious gift.

—Kate DiCamillo

Crucial to this book is the premise that teachers use Universal Design for Learning techniques for all literacy activities allowing access to all. "According to the most recent data from the U.S. Department of Education, 81 percent of the high school class of 2013 graduated with a regular diploma, marking several years of improvement for the nation as a whole and a large majority of states. With a graduation rate of only 62% students with disabilities lag considerably behind their peers" (http://www.edweek.org/ew/toc/2015/06/04/index.html). Reading and writing well are essential to the literacy needs of every ability level.

What types of strategies can teachers use to facilitate reading and writing for all learners? The Center for Applied Special Technology (CAST) defines Universal Design for Learning as "a set of principles for curriculum development that gives all individuals equal opportunities to learn. UDL provides a blueprint for creating instructional goals, methods, materials, and assessments that work for everyone—not a single, one-size-fits-all solution but rather flexible approaches that can be customized and adjusted for individual needs" (http://www.cast.org/udl).

MULTIPLE MEANS OF REPRESENTATION

The three guiding principles of Universal Design for Learning provide a framework for meeting the needs of all learners (Hallahan, Kauffman, & Pullen, 2015). The first principle is "multiple means of representation." Students' learning styles vary. One way teachers can ensure that all students have access to literacy learning is to use a multisensory instructional approach. Teachers can present lessons incorporating visual, auditory, and kinesthetic components (Rowsell & Kendrick, 2013; Spires, Hervey, Morris, & Stelpflug, 2012). Although this may sound complicated, it simply involves teachers being cognizant of incorporating these aspects in their teaching by consistently asking, "What visuals will I use in this lesson? What is the auditory component in this lesson? What is the kinesthetic component of my lesson?" This simple adaptation in teaching style may facilitate learning for a multitude of learners.

For example, we know that our students with autism spectrum disorder are visual learners. By using a multisensory approach, the visual component to the lesson is automatically met. This also assists English Language Learners. Visually impaired students need an auditory component in order to learn. Students identified as having attention-deficit/hyperactivity disorder may benefit from using some form of physical activity in order to learn. The teacher using a multisensory instructional approach automatically facilitates these students' needs. Students with learning disabilities have a variety of learning styles depending on the nature of the learning disability. Again, according to CAST,

> Learning is impossible if information is imperceptible to the learner, and difficult when information is presented in formats that require extraordinary effort or assistance. To reduce barriers to learning, it is important to ensure that key information is equally perceptible to all learners by: 1) providing the same information through different modalities (e.g., through vision, hearing, or touch); 2) providing information in a format that will allow for adjustability by the user (e.g., text that can be enlarged, sounds that can be amplified). Such multiple representations not only ensure that information is accessible to learners with particular sensory and perceptual disabilities, but also easier to access and comprehend for many others. (http://www.cast.org/udl)

MULTIPLE MEANS OF ACTION AND EXPRESSION

The second principle of Universal Design for Learning is "multiple means of action and expression." Teachers may use technology in a multitude of ways in order to scaffold literacy and communication in the twenty-first century, and their opportunities grow and change on a daily basis (Lewis, Charron, Clamp, & Craig, 2016). It is the teacher's job to stay abreast of new technologies.

Asking the following questions guides teachers in their technology choices:

- Would any students benefit from listening to this text on tape/DVD?
- What students require a specific literacy program in order to be successful?
- How can this concept be presented?

For example, the *Read, Write, Gold* program from TextHelp facilitates students' reading and writing. Students may highlight any text or online websites, and the text will be read out loud for them. Along with numerous editing tools, there is an MP3 converter that turns voice into text. There is also a voice dictation tool. Students require direct instruction in how to use this tool, but using the Gradual Release of Responsibility model eventually leads to independence with the software. Google "Gradual Release of Responsibility" for visual images.

WebAIM offers numerous ideas for assisting students with motor deficits. Camera Mouse allows students to control the mouse by moving their head. Tech Matrix is a wonderful resource for educators working with students with disabilities. All of these facilitate students' reading and writing skills.

Presentation options are vast. PowerPoint presentation? Prezi presentation? Sometimes a comic strip (Fink, 2012) or video may be best for specific children. Students can make a drawing or a sketch using the Kerproof website. Animoto and SAM Animation allow students to make videos and movies. What about making a captioned movie? The possibilities are truly endless.

MULTIPLE MEANS OF ENGAGEMENT

The third principle of Universal Design for Learning is "multiple means of engagement." Student engagement is a prerequisite for any literacy learning to take place. How can teachers ensure that students are engaged in reading and writing activities? Teachers need to ask themselves for each and every writing assignment done in class, "How can I teach and have students practice this writing concept in an engaging manner?" Using authentic writing experiences, such as writing to a pen pal, writing an advertisement for a newspaper or for television, writing a newspaper or magazine article, or writing an article to post on a school website, may motivate students much more than completing a required writing prompt developed by a teacher. Meaningful writing is motivating to all students.

Choice is another motivator. Even providing a choice of prompts may be more motivating for students than providing students with only *one* writing prompt. Again, teachers need to ask questions before every reading and writing assignment. Can the writing activity be achieved through writing a play, a poem, a children's book, or an advertisement? "What choices can I give my students for this particular written language assignment? Should this be an individual assignment, or could students work in peer or small groups?" For some students, group or peer work is a wonderful motivator (Lindstrom & Drolet, 2017). This particularly aids English Language Learners with language development.

Although this book is about improving students' written language, there are a variety of ways to express oneself using written language. Students *must* learn to write. However, they should be allowed choice in *how* they choose to write. This may encompass using a pen and paper, a computer, or a speech recognition system that translates talk into written language.

Students must also be allowed the time to write, and the amount of time will vary from individual to individual. This may involve keeping writing "open" for students to return to whenever there is free time in the classroom. This may mean reducing the quantity of writing required for some individuals. Reducing the length of an assignment may be the only accommodation needed by a specific student.

Dividing a written assignment into specific sections may aid a student in better understanding the time commitments necessary to successfully complete a written language assignment. A checklist with due dates may be all the support necessary for students with time management challenges. A similar checklist may provide a list of safe websites students may visit to obtain information about a writing topic. Again, levels of support will vary for each individual student.

Students also organize their thoughts in different ways. Graphic organizers assist all students in organizing their thoughts. However, students require different degrees of assistance in learning how to effectively use them. Some students can listen to a five-minute explanation of how to use a graphic organizer and then use it effectively. Others may need to practice using a variety of graphic organizers with teacher assistance before finding the one that works best for them. Some may require extensive support in learning to use one type of graphic organizer before being able to use it effectively. Organizers can be adapted to meet each individual's needs. The following website offers numerous options: http://www.dailyteachingtools.com/free-graphic-organizers.html. Many times, these planners will effectively scaffold students who are achieving many years below grade level.

Teachers in a variety of classrooms can use the ideas presented in this book. The majority of students will be successful simply using the Universal Design for Learning model and associated methodology. However, there will be a few students who will require more extensive accommodations or modifications.

The teacher's role is to offer adaptations to the entire class and allow those students who will benefit the opportunity to use them. Letting all learners know *why* it is important to understand particular concepts and providing them the strategies they require in order to be successful in their learning using authentic motivational topics and materials ensures success for the entire class. Teachers must raise the level of literacy for all students.

7

Reading and Reflecting on One's Own Writing

We do not learn from experience . . . we learn from reflecting on experience.

—John Dewey

By building deliberate connections between student reading and writing, teachers encourage students to make their own choices. This ownership empowers student writers. They merge minds with the writers that they have read (Graham & Hebert, 2010). They may or may not agree with every writer, but they begin to recognize a common pursuit, and they learn to understand and appreciate the power of the written word. Students need to be able to read their own writing critically. They need to apply their reading skills by writing for a reader. We critique others' writing all the time and decide quite early what we wish to emulate and what we don't. By reading critically, we sharpen our skills and develop our taste in writing. This is the process by which we critique others' and our own developing but still-deficient writing.

Fairly early in their reading/writing careers, it is good to allow students themselves to select and then attempt to critically analyze excerpts of text. By asking them to find a paragraph or page they think is significant, interesting, or exemplary and then explain why they chose it, the value of the mentor text is expanded. Instead of always providing them with *our* idea of what is exemplary, we ask them to find something in a text that *they* like and then verbalize what they noticed and why they think it is good. Their critical thinking is nurtured and challenged. Are there key word choices the writer has made? Are there sentences that seem tailor-made for their purpose? Are details clearly selected for effect? Whether or not the student has the skill to determine the possible or actual purpose of a writer's choices, the fact that he or she stopped to notice and ask what is going on is important and worth the discussion. Perhaps the class, with the teacher's guidance, can help.

WRITING RUBRICS—FOR STUDENTS, WITH STUDENTS

Teachers should use assessment systems that encourage student writers and challenge them to improve. First, we develop specific rubrics together with students that are designed around the writing task. We begin with a question: What are the qualities of an excellent paper written for this purpose? Collect students' thinking on the board, judging no one's contribution. Allow students to recognize ideas that are similar and can be merged. Help them recognize specific traits of writing that are appropriate to this particular assignment or purpose. Work to narrow attributes to five or six categories.

Help students recognize that the purpose of their writing will dictate the elements of a rubric. Is providing evidence important? Should the writer give examples? Is originality or creativity important to the success of this piece? Once you have collected descriptions of the most important elements, have them help you assign maximum scores for each attribute. Retain their language as much as you can without sacrificing the common vocabulary you have worked to establish as a class. Then revise the rubric and distribute with the topic or the prompt at the top for each student so that as they write they can consider the stated attributes of an excellent paper.

It will be different for each assignment, some valuing evidence, others requiring quotations and reference, and still others valuing creativity more highly. Leave at least one-third of the paper blank for comments and encouragement. By building reflective practices into the rubric, we let students know that the learning is not over when the paper is finished. We read and consider our own work.

RUBRIC FOR REMEMBERING AN EVENT

_____ (15) Clear, well-focused topic and convincing and skillful development of the central idea. Imaginative and interesting approach that considers the audience.

_____ (15) Topic and its development are personal, significant, and universal in appeal.

_____ (15) Unified, coherent organization. Effective paragraphing and smooth transitions between ideas and paragraphs. Distinct introduction, body, and conclusion.

_____ (15) Vivid, vigorous diction. Lively and well-chosen detail. Imagery enhances the meaning and appeals to the senses. If featured, dialogue contributes to development of plot and character.

_____ (15) Varied, appropriate, and correct sentence structure. Voice and style are distinctive and personal.

_____ (15) Few or no mechanical errors relative to the complexity and length (spelling, punctuation, capitalization, and grammar).

_____ (10) Process is fully documented. Presentation is effective and complete and adheres to the format of the Modern Language Association (MLA). All materials have been submitted on time.

Grade: _____

Comments:

RUBRIC FOR ARGUING A POSITION

_____ (15) Writer takes a clear position on an issue that is arguable and with which reasonable people might disagree. Thesis is original and thought provoking.

_____ (15) Writer gives plausible reasons and provides convincing support for the position. Writer anticipates opposing arguments or objections.

_____ (15) The paper has unified, coherent organization, exhibiting effective paragraphing and smooth transitions between ideas, creating a logical framework.

_____ (15) Writer shows command of the language, including vivid, vigorous diction and well-chosen detail. The work is interesting as well as persuasive. Voice and style are distinctive and personal.

_____ (15) Varied, appropriate, and correct sentence structure. Few or no mechanical errors relative to the complexity and length (spelling, punctuation, capitalization, and grammar).

_____ (15) Research is documented both in text and in a Works Cited page, according to MLA guidelines. Sources are reliable and well chosen.

_____ (10) Process is fully documented with drafts and reflection on process. Presentation is complete and on time.

Grade: _____

Comments:

RUBRIC FOR WRITING ABOUT READING

_____ (10) Demonstrates a clear understanding of the meaning of the piece.

_____ (10) Evaluates elements of form by identifying some of the author's artistic and strategic choices, possibly including diction, imagery, detail, language, and syntax. Discusses how formal elements support meaning. Supports points with quotes and examples from text.

_____ Grade

A grade of 20 indicates excellence in both what you said and how you said it.

Comments:

ASSESSMENT

When students have a written assignment to turn in, require that they order the pages, from back to front, as follows: 1) the prewriting activity or earliest thinking; 2) a draft that was shared with a peer, with comments; 3) a final, edited draft; and 4) the rubric sheet, ready for your teacher assessment and your comments.

But we are not done until the reflection is added. This will be handwritten and attached to the package. A reflection documents the learning.

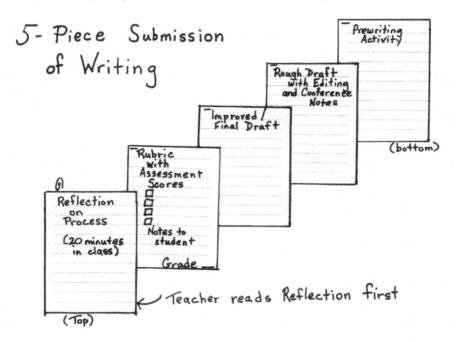

INVITE METACOGNITIVE THINKING

Structure reflections for each writing assignment by choosing relevant and interesting questions. Well-chosen questions will often bring to the forefront the unique requirements of the purpose of this piece. If it's an argument, some questions will result in a deeper understanding of the nature and structure of a good argument. If it's a literary analysis, other factors should be reviewed and expressed on both the rubric and the reflection. Fifteen or twenty minutes of consideration mark the end of the process as the student offers his or her paper for teacher perusal and assessment.

A good motivational incentive for thoughtful reflection might be worth 5 or 10 percent of the total grade. Make reflection a regular part of classroom practice. Through written reflection, we recognize the recursive processes of good writing:

from reading others' writing to writing our own, from rereading to rewriting, and from consideration of the process of our writing to writing the reflection. In each step of the process, we sow seeds for improvement.

The following list of questions for reflection can help target various skills and understandings to encourage the metacognitive process. These questions call on the deeper processes of both reading and writing. The response time for a question should be approximately 15 minutes, as some reading and thinking are involved. Some students with processing speed disorders may benefit from receiving these questions a day ahead of time as well as verbally discussing them with a peer, teacher, or aide.

QUESTIONS FOR REFLECTION

- How did you choose your topic?
- Explain and defend your choice of title. Did you consider others?
- Who is your audience? What response do you expect from your audience?
- What did you do in your writing to appeal to your particular audience?
- Defend the order of your paper. Did you consider an alternative order?
- Copy your first sentence to this page. Why is a good beginning? Do the same with your last sentence. Will your words be effective with a reader?
- Find and copy your best statement of thesis or idea. How does it relate to your purpose in writing?
- Copy your strongest, best-constructed sentence. How did you structure it *for effect*?
- Describe your tone. Which words did you use that convey your attitude toward your subject, your opinion, or your audience?
- What was your most difficult problem in writing this piece? How did you address the problem?
- How satisfied are you with the result of your writing? What might you have done differently?
- List three to five words you used that you think were excellent choices (diction). Evaluate how they were placed in each sentence. How are diction and syntax related?
- Copy two sentences whose structures are well considered (syntax). Show how each construction supports your overall meaning.
- Did you choose to employ imagery to reinforce your point or purpose? If yes, how does it operate? If no, consider now how you might appeal to the senses and use figurative language to strengthen your writing.
- How did you choose detail to support your meaning? List effective details. For each, consider what it ultimately adds to meaning.
- Did you confer with anyone about this paper? With whom? What advice did you receive? What did you decide to do about that advice?

- What processes, at this point, do you consider most helpful to your successful writing?
- What grammatical problems have you had? How did you address your problem(s) in this piece?
- Find three verbs you might strengthen. Write a possible replacement in the margin next to each one.
- Looking at any page of your paper, what sentence structure do you favor (simple, compound, complex, compound–complex, questions, and so on)?
- What sentence length do you favor (long, intermediate, or short)? Find a sentence that might be a candidate for improvement. How could it be varied for effect?

A TEACHER/COACH'S RESPONSE TO THE STUDENT WRITER

When a writer falls short, we have shared measures to use to describe deficiencies or gaps based on our rubric and the writer's description of his or her own process to support, advise, and encourage a writer's improvement. After all, all of us—both teachers and students—are striving to be better writers. Like a good golfer, we compete against others but even more against our own past performance. In the middle and high school classroom, we have an opportunity to advance our common thinking and our skills by joining the safe and supportive reading and writing community. Once we leave the school, we can enter into the larger literate community and join the adult cultural and intellectual discussion. Will our students be ready?

Self-assessment in the course of writing can encourage students to take pride of ownership in their writing. Teachers can extend the discussion of "What makes writing great?" into the class construction of a rubric when we approach a writing task or when we are engaged in editing once we have a grasp on the purpose of our assignment. The purpose of assessment shouldn't be the grade but rather the improvement of each young writer. Students have more buy-in when they help construct the rubric.

When students hand in their papers, complete with all drafts including a reflection on their writing process, staple the rubric page on top. Keep it simple and leave lots of space for written encouragement. What is good about this paper? What next steps might this writer take? Ruth Culham's (2003) *6 + 1 Traits of Writing* offers an excellent collection of supportive and constructive comments for writers on the general categories most often found in adopted rubrics (see also Culham 2010, 2014). Some students may require visuals included in the rubric to better ensure understanding. Rubric descriptions should be in the students' own words, again to make sure that students comprehend the rubric vocabulary.

MORE PRACTICE FOR STUDENT ASSESSORS

Students will benefit from practice assessing anonymous sample papers. This could be organized in a number of ways: round-robin, reading with a partner, or small group. Students rate each paper's traits and then compare their assessments with those of others. This practice puts them in the assessor's chair, giving them a fresh look at what good or not-so-good writing looks like. They will be more critical of their own work—critical in a positive way!

8

Closing the Literacy Loop

> The reality of a serious writer is a reality of many voices, some of them belonging
> to the writer, some of them belonging to the world of readers at large.
>
> —Aberjhani

To write is to create meaning for oneself and others using words. To read is to see
and understand someone else's experience and perspective interpreted through one's
own lens. The written word can be shared with another literate human being. It can
also be a means of saving one's thoughts for another time or place. Both reading
and writing should be empowering. Teachers need to help students see the limitless
possibilities and motivate them to hone their skills. Although writers also write to
please themselves, writing is inherently a social activity. Writing implies that there is
a reader. Louise Rosenblatt's (1978) idea that it is a "transaction" is apt: one writes,
capturing a thought or experience in a certain time and place, and then releases it,
thereby potentially altering a reader's thought or experience in an entirely different
time and place.

Writers need to have a purpose for their writing. This purpose may be for personal
enjoyment, to persuade others in their thinking or actions, or to communicate with
others. It is important, however, to note that a writer's purpose is directly connected
to the writer's audience, whether it be the author him- or herself or the world at
large. Being a writer gives an individual power to impart thoughts to others and to
influence others' thinking. Writers who twenty years ago would have had no access
to a publisher or spreading ideas worldwide now can become overnight authors via
the Internet.

Writing is empowering, and the message of empowerment should be imparted
to every student: How can *your* writing make a difference in *your* life? Will your
personal writing positively affect your mental health (diaries)? Will your persuasive

writing change a school policy? City policy? Extend your curfew time? Convince your coach to give you more playing time? Will your informational writing positively affect your grade in a class? Students too often see their only audience in their teacher, who can be viewed by students as judge and jury.

Having a purpose for writing motivates all students and makes the time it takes to write worth taking. When students understand that "writing is power," the act of writing takes on a positive perspective, and that perspective leads to writing production and personal gratification. The motivation inherent in the task promotes writing development over time.

Assuming that the above is true, how do teachers foster *positive gains in writing*? By giving students *choice* in what they write, by giving students *time* to do their writing, and by using *authentic* writing activities that students will use when they become adults. No matter how old we are, we all struggle to find meaning in our life and experience. Each word a writer selects represents a new opportunity to infuse meaning. Each choice is significant as long as the writer is deliberate and cares about the message. If we regularly call attention to the art found in our reading, students will learn to take more care in their writing.

As writers, teachers, and learners, we continually strive to improve. Throughout our lives, we will *read* in order to *write effectively and well*:

- We read because we seek to know and then to share our knowledge with others.
- We seek to understand so that we can share and teach ways in which our students and others will learn regardless of our own preferred ways of knowing and understanding.
- We seek to find ways in which we and our students can apply our knowledge and understanding to solve problems and be useful at a basic level and beyond.
- We seek to know and to understand as a springboard and/or scaffold, to accept the higher-level challenge.
- We will break down problems to understand the *why* and the *how*, going beyond the superficial approach, in order to find ways of expressing and solving more complex problems.
- Together, we seek to build a thoughtful and analytical process by which we measure and evaluate what is best and worthy.

The process of writing, as in reading, is ultimately *ethical*. Evaluation of every choice a writer can make involves more than skill. It also assigns worth. We define ourselves as we engage in the process of describing, analyzing, and valuing, in every word we choose and every idea we verbally construct. Through reading and writing, literate people connect with and interpret themselves and their world.

References

BOOKS/ARTICLES

ACT. (2011). *The condition of college and career readiness.* Iowa City, IA: Author. Retrieved from http://www.act.org/research/policymakers/cccr11/pdf/Condition of College and Career Readiness 2011.pdf

Adoff, A., & Andrews, B. (1968). *I am the darker brother: An anthology of modern poems by Negro Americans.* New York: Macmillan.

Allen, J. (2005). *Reading history: A practical guide to improving literacy.* New York: Oxford University Press.

Allen, J. (2007). *Inside words: Tools for teaching academic vocabulary grades 4–12.* Portland, ME: Stenhouse.

Allen, J. (2008). *More tools for teaching content literacy.* Portland, ME: Stenhouse.

Allington, R. (2011). *What really matters for struggling readers: Designing research based programs.* Boston: Pearson/Allyn & Bacon.

Assaf, L., Ash, G., Saunders, J., & Johnson, J. (2011). Renewing two seminal literacy practices: I-Charts and I-Search papers. *English Journal, 18*(4), 31–42.

Barry, A. (2012). "I was skeptical at first": Content literacy in the art museum. *Journal of Adolescent and Adult Literacy, 55*(7), 597–607.

Biancarosa, C., & Snow, C. E. (2006). *Reading next—A vision for action and research in middle and high school literacy: A report to Carnegie Corporation of New York* (2nd ed.). Washington, DC: Alliance for Excellent Education.

Bloom, B. (1976). *Human characteristics and school learning.* New York: McGraw-Hill. Retrieved from https://nbccffcoach.wikispaces.com/file/view/Revised+Bloom's+Taxonomy .pdf

Bush, V. C. (Ed.). (2002). *Believe me, I know.* San Francisco: Writers Corps Books.

Casey, G. (2013). Interdisciplinary literacy through social media in the mathematics classroom: An action research study. *Journal of Adolescent and Adult Literacy, 57*(1), 60–71.

Charron, N. (2007). I learned that there's a state called Victoria. *The Reading Teacher, 60*(8), 762–769.

Charron, N., Fenton, M., Harris, M., & Procek, C. (2012). Encouraging struggling writers K–12: Practical ideas from practicing practitioners. *New England Reading Association Journal, 48*(1), 66–72.

Collins, S. (2008). *The hunger games.* New York: Scholastic.

Constable, S., Grossi, B., Moniz, A., & Ryan, L. (2013). Meeting the common core standards for students with autism: The challenge for educators. *Teaching Exceptional Children, 45*(3), 7–13.]

Culham, R. (2003). *6 + 1 traits of writing: The complete guide.* New York: Scholastic.

Culham, R. (2010). *Traits of writing: The complete guide for middle school.* New York: Scholastic.

Culham, R. (2014). *The writing thief: Using mentor texts to teach the craft of writing.* New York: Scholastic.

Curtis, C. P. (1999). *Bud, not Buddy.* New York: Delacorte Press.

Daniels, H. (2002). *Literature circles: Voice and choice in book clubs and reading groups.* Portland, ME: Stenhouse.

Dillard, A. (1987). *An American childhood* (Large Print ed.). New York: Harper & Row.

Fang, Z. (2014). Preparing content area teachers for disciplinary literacy instruction. *Journal of Adolescent and Adult Literacy, 57*(6), 444–448. doi:10.1002/jaal.269

Fenton, M., & Charron, N. (2016). Critical thinking through language acquisition and development: An instructional model. *New England Reading Association Journal, 51*(2), 1–8.

Fink, L. (2012).Using comic strips as a book report alternative. *The Reading Teacher, 66*(2), 88–164.

Fisher, D., & Frey, N. (2014). Close reading as an intervention for struggling middle school readers. *Journal of Adolescent and Adult Literacy, 57*(5), 367–376. *doi:*10.1002/jaal.266

Fleishman, P. (1988) *Joyful noise: Poems for two voices.* New York: HarperCollins.

Gallagher, K. (2009). *Article of the week.* Portland, ME: Stenhouse.

Gallagher, K. (2011). *Write like this: Teaching real-world writing through modeling and mentor texts.* Portland, ME: Stenhouse.

Goodwin, B., & Miller, K. (2012/2013). Nonfiction reading promotes student success. *Educational Leadership, 70*(4), 80–82.

Graham, S., & Hebert, M. (2010). *Writing to read: Evidence of how writing can improve reading.* New York: Carnegie Corporation of New York. Retrieved from https://www.carnegie.org/media/filer_public/9d/e2/9de20604-a055-42da-bc00-77da949b29d7/ccny_report_2010_writing.pdf

Guthrie, J., & Klauda, S. (2014). Effects of classroom practices on reading comprehension, engagement, and motivations for adolescents. *Reading Research Quarterly, 49*(4), 387–416. *doi:*10.1002/rrq.81

Guthrie, J., McRae, A., & Klauda, S. (2007). Contributions of concept-oriented reading instruction to knowledge about interventions for motivations in reading. *Educational Psychologist, 42*(4), 237–250. doi:10.1080/00461520701621087

Guthrie, J. T., Wigfield, A., Humenick, N. M., Perencevich, K. C., Taboada, A., & Barbosa, P. (2006). Influences of stimulating tasks on reading motivation and comprehension. *Journal of Educational Research, 99*(4), 232–245.

Guthrie, J. T., Wigfield, A., & VonSecker, C. (2000). Integrated instruction on motivation and strategy use in reading. *Journal of Educational Psychology, 92*(2), 331–341.

Hallahan, D. P., Kauffman, J. M., & Pullen, P. C. (2015). *Exceptional Learners: An Introduction to Special Education* (13th ed.). Pearson Education.

Harvey, S., & Goudvis, A. (2007). *Strategies that work; Teaching comprehension for understanding and engagement.* Portland, ME: Stenhouse.

Hesse, K. (1997). *Out of the dust.* New York: Scholastic.

Huxley, A. (1959). *Collected essays.* New York: Harper & Brothers.

King, S. (2000). *On writing: A memoir of the craft.* New York: Scribner.

Lesh, B. A. (2011). *Why won't you just tell us the answer?* Portland, ME: Stenhouse.

Levine, S. (2014). Making interpretation visible with an affect-based strategy. *Reading Research Quarterly, 49(3),* 283–303.

Lewis, L., Charron, N., Clamp, C., & Craig, M. (2016). Co-robot therapy to foster social skills in special need learners: Three pilot studies. In M. Caporuscio, F. De la Prieta, T. Di Mascio, R. Gennari, J. Rodriguez, & P. Vittorini (Eds.), *Methodologies and intelligent systems for technology enhanced learning* (pp. 131–141). Basel: Springer.

Lindstrom, C., & Drolet, B. M. (2017). *What's missing: Best practices for teaching students with disabilities.* Lanham, MD: Rowman & Littlefield

Macrorie, K. (1988). *The I-search paper.* New York: Heinemann. (Original work published 1980)

Martinez, M. G., Yokota, J., & Temple, C. (2017). *Thinking and learning through children's literature.* Lanham, MD: Rowman & Littlefield.

Miller, A. (1971). *The portable Arthur Miller.* New York: Viking.

Milo, G. (2017). *Rebooting social studies: Strategies for reimagining history classes.* Lanham, MD: Rowman & Littlefield.

Monahan, M. (2013). Writing voiced arguments. *Journal of Adolescent and Adult Literacy, 57*(1), 31–40.

Morse, O. (n.d.). *SOAPSTone.* http://apcentral.collegeboard.com/apc/public/preap/teachers_corner/45200.html

National Research Council. (2004). *Engaging schools: Fostering high school students' motivation to learn.* Washington, DC: National Academies Press.

Norman, R., & Roberts, K. (2013). Not just pretty pictures. *Educational Leadership, 71*(3), 62–66.

Nye, N. S. (2010). *Time you let me in: 25 poets under 25.* New York: Greenwillow Books.

Olson, C. B. (2011). *The reading/writing connection: Strategies for teaching and learning in the secondary classroom.* Boston: Pearson.

Pearson, P. D., & Gallagher, M. C. (1983). The instruction of reading comprehension. *Contemporary Educational Psychology, 8,* 317–344.

Porter, P. P. (2005). *The crazy man.* Toronto: Groundwood Books.

Robertson, D. A., Ford-Connors, E., & Dougherty, S. M. (2017). *Engaging readers: Supporting all students in knowledge-driven reading, grades 4–8.* Lanham, MD: Rowman & Littlefield.

Rohrer, D., Taylor, K., Pashler, H., Wixted, J. T., & Cepeda, N. J. (2005). The effect of overlearning on long-term retention. *Applied Cognitive Psychology, 19*(3), 361–374.

Rosenblatt, L. (1978). *The reader, the text, the poem: The transactional theory of the literary work.* Carbondale: Southern Illinois University Press.

Rowsell, J., & Kendrick, M. (2013). Boys' hidden literacies: The critical need for the visual. *Journal of Adolescent and Adult Literacy, 56*(7), 587–599.

Ryan, P. M. (2000). *Esperanza rising.* New York: Scholastic.

Schunk, D. H. (2003). Self-efficacy for reading and writing: Influence of modeling, goal setting, and self-evaluation. *Reading and Writing Quarterly, 19*, 159–172.

Schunk, D. H., & Rice, J. M. (1993). Strategy fading and progress feedback: Effects on self-efficacy and comprehension among students receiving remedial reading services. *Journal of Special Education, 27*, 257–276.

Schur, J. B. (2007). *Eyewitness to the past: Strategies for teaching American history in grades 5–12.* Portland, ME: Stenhouse.

Self, Elliott. (2013). Ten reasons art education matters. *Education Update, 55*(1), 1–4.5.

Shapiro, A. (2012). *Night of the republic.* New York: Houghton Mifflin Harcourt.

Spires, H. A., Hervey, L. G., Morris, G., & Stelpflug, C. (2012). Energizing project-based inquiry: Middle-grade students read, write, and create videos. *Journal of Adolescent and Adult Literacy, 55*(6), 483.

Tovani, C. (2000). *I read it, but I don't get it: Comprehension strategies for adolescent readers.* Portland, ME: Stenhouse.

Vygotsky, L. (1997). *Thought and language* (A. Kozulin, Trans.). Cambridge, MA: MIT Press. (Original work published 1934)

Walker, A. (2003). *In love and trouble: Stories of clack women.* New York: Harcourt Brace Jovanovich.

Wilhelm, J. D. (2007). *Engaging readers and writers with inquiry: Promoting deep understandings in language arts and the content areas with guiding questions.* New York: Scholastic.

Wilhelm, J. D. (2016). *You gotta be the book: Teaching engaged and reflective reading with adolescents.* New York: Teachers College Press.

Yolen, J. (2002). *Wild wings.* Honesdale, PA: Boyds Mill Press.

Yolen, J. (2003). *Once upon ice: And other frozen poems.* Honesdale, PA: Boyds Mill Press.

Yolen, J. (2010). *An egret's day.* Honesdale, PA: Boyds Mill Press.

LINKS

A Chronology of U.S. historical documents. (n.d.). http://www.law.ou.edu/hist

Acrostic Poems. (n.d.). http://www.readwritethink.org/classroom-resources/student-interactives/acrostic-poems-30045.html

Angelou, M. (n.d.). http://www.poets.org/poetsorg/poem/still-i-rise

Bloom's Taxonomy (n.d.). http://buhlercc.wikispaces.com/Bloom%27s+Taxonomy

Brockton High School (n.d.). http://www.agi.harvard.edu/events/2009Conference/2009AGI ConferenceReport6-30-2010web.pdf

Carmichael, S. (n.d.). Stairway to heaven: Examining metaphor in popular music. http://www.readwritethink.org/classroom-resources/lesson-plans/stairway-heaven-examining-metaphor-975.html

Civil War. (n.d.). http://www.civilwar.org/education/history/primarysources

Common Core State Standards. (n.d.).http://www.corestandards.org/other.../key-shifts-in-english-language-arts

Cox, A. K., & Jenkins, A. (n.d.). Swish! Pow! Whack! Teaching onomatopoeia through sports poetry. http://www.readwritethink.org/classroom-resources/lesson-plans/swish-whack-teaching-onomatopoeia-1131.html

cummings, e.e. (n.d.). http://www.youtube.com/watch?v=NA836Ax7scw; http://www.poetry foundation.org/poem/176657

Diamante Poems. (n.d.). http://www.readwritethink.org/classroom-resources/student-interactives/diamante-poems-30053.html

Donne, J. (n.d.). No man is an island. http://web.cs.dal.ca/~johnston/poetry/island.html

Environmental Protection Agency. (n.d.). http://www2.epa.gov/learn-issues

Epals. (n.d.). http://www.epals.com/#!/main

Essay Writing. (n.d.). http://www.readwritethink.org/classroom-resources/student-interactives/essay-30063.html

Essential Questions. (n.d.). https://www.gilderlehrman.org

Filkins, S. (n.d.). Promoting student-directed inquiry with the i-search paper. http://www.readwritethink.org/professional-development/strategy-guides/promoting-student-directed-inquiry-30783.html

Fishbowl. (n.d.). https://www.facinghistory.org/for-educators/educator-resources/teaching-strategy/fishbowl and https://www.learner.org/workshops/tml/workshop3/teaching2.html

Florida Assessments for Instruction in Reading. (2010). http://www.fcrr.org/FAIR_Search_Tool/FAIR_Search_Tool.aspx

Graffiti Wall. (n.d.). http://www.readwritethink.org/classroom-resources/lesson-plans/graffiti-wall-discussing-responding-208.html

Graphic Organizers (n.d.). http://www.readingrockets.org/article/52137; http://www.readwritethink.org/classroom-resources/student-interactives

Hardy, T. (n.d.). The convergence of the twain. http://www.poetryfoundation.org/poem/176678

Historic Newsreel Footage of the Cuban Missile Crisis. (n.d.). http://www.smithsonianmag.com/videos/category/3play_1/historic-newsreel-footage-of-the-cuban-missi/?no-ist

History: Science and Medicine. (2015, April 7). http://guides.lib.washington.edu/content.php?pid=72468&sid=653510

Hughes, L. (n.d.). A dream deferred. http://www.cswnet.com/~menamc/langston.htm

Hughes, L. (n.d.). Freedom's plow. http://www.poemhunter.com/poem/freedom-s-plow

Inferences Worksheets. (n.d.). http://www.ereadingworksheets.com/free-reading-worksheets/reading-comprehension-worksheets/inferences-worksheets

Interactive Journal Writing. (n.d.). http://edu.glogster.com/?ref=com

Journal Writing. (n.d.). https://penzu.com/

Katz, H. (2012, May). Civil War battlefield art. http://ngm.nationalgeographic.com/2012/05/civil-war-sketches/katz-text

Key, F. S. (n.d.). The Star Spangled Banner. http://www.scoutsongs.com/lyrics/starspangledbanner.html

Lanier, S. (n.d.). The Battle of Lexington. http://www.poetry-archive.com/l/the_battle_of_lexington.html

Lassonde, C. A. (n.d.). Using THIEVES to preview nonfiction texts. http://www.readwritethink.org/classroom-resources/lesson-plans/using-thieves-preview-nonfiction-112.html

Longfellow, H. W. (n.d.). Paul Revere's ride. http://www.poets.org/poetsorg/poem/paul-reveres-ride

Math-Science Notebooks. (n.d.). http://interactive-math-science-notebooks.wikispaces.com

Meinke, J. P. (n.d.). Advice to my son. http://www.ifreeman.com/freeman/advicetomyson.htm

Music. (n.d.). http://www.youtube.com/watch?v=Ec_pDV07pQg

NAEA Learning. (2015). http://www.arteducators.org/learning

National Geographic. (n.d.). http://education.nationalgeographic.com/education/?ar_a=1

National Science Teachers Association. (n.d.). http://www.nsta.org/publications/news/story .aspx?id=57384

https://www.nichd.nih.gov/publications/pubs/nrp/Documents/report.pdf

Once More to the Lake. (n.d.). http://wheretheclassroomends.com/wp-content/ uploads/2013/07/White_OnceMoretotheLake1.pdf

Poems and Poets of Today and the First World War. (n.d.). http://www.warpoetry.co.uk

Poetry: Maggie and Molly. (n.d.). http://www.youtube.com/watch?v=PZ_06r0OGR4

Public Radio. (n.d.). http://writersalmanac.publicradio.org/index.php?date=2002/03/07

Reading. (n.d.). http://wiki.theplaz.com/w/images/6-Getting_Caught_Reading.pdf

Resources: Student Activities. (n.d.). http://americanart.si.edu/education/resources/activities

Roosevelt, F. D. (1933, March 4). The New Deal in action. http://www.fdrlibrary.marist .edu/archives/resources/newdealprojects.html; http://www.archives.gov/education/lessons/ fdr-fireside

Roosevelt's Day of Infamy Speech. (n.d.). http://education.nationalgeographic.com/education/ media/roosevelts-day-infamy-speech/?ar_a=1

Scaffolding. (n.d.). http://pubs.cde.ca.gov/tcsii/ch2/scaffolding.aspx

Science and Invention. (n.d.). http://www.loc.gov/teachers/classroommaterials/themes/science/ set.html

Science Journals. (n.d.). http://www.nsta.org/publications/news/story.aspx?id=51882

1790 Census. (n.d.). http://education.nationalgeographic.com/education/media/ us-census-1790/?ar_a=1

Shapiro, D. (2010, May 11). Enhancing learning with science notebooks. http://www.nsta .org/publications/news/story.aspx?id=57384

Slave Sale. (n.d.). http://education.nationalgeographic.com/education/media/ slave-sale/?ar_a=1

Smithsonian Institution. (n.d.). http://www.smithsonianeducation.org/educators

Socratic Seminar. (n.d.). https://www.nwabr.org/sites/default/files/SocSem.pdf; http://www .readwritethink.org/professional-development/strategy-guides/socratic-seminars-30600. html

Students and Science. (n.d.). https://student.societyforscience.org

(n.d.). https://www.google.com/search?client=safari&rls=en&q=To+Kill+a+Mockingbird+Socratic+ Seminar.doc&ie=UTF-8&oe=UTF-8

Tennyson, A. (n.d.). The-Eagle. http://allpoetry.com/The-Eagle

Transition Words. (n.d.). http://www.smart-words.org/linking-words/transition-words.html)

The 12 Principles of Paideia Philosophy. (n.d.). https://www.paideia.org/about-paideia/ philosophy

Universal Design for Learning. (n.d.). http://www.cast.org/udl/index.html

Venn Diagram Introduction. (n.d.). http://www.classtools.net/education-games-php/ venn_intro

Voice. (n.d.). https://www.google.com/search?q=passive+vs.+active+voice&ie=utf-8&oe=utf-8 #q=passive+vs.+active+voice+for+elementary+school

Whitman, W. (n.d.). O captain! My captain! http://www.poetryfoundation.org/poem/174742

Wordles. (n.d.). http://www.wordle.net" www.wordle.net

Wordsworth, W. (n.d.). The daffodils. http://www.poets.org/poetsorg/poem/daffodils

Writing a Historical Poem. (n.d.). http://www.pbs.org/opb/historydetectives/educators/ technique-guide/writing-an-historical-poem

About the Authors

Nancy Charron attended the University of Michigan and received a bachelor of science degree in elementary education and deaf education. She received a master of education degree in teaching reading from Western Michigan University and a doctorate degree in language arts and literacy from the University of Massachusetts. She has worked in different capacities at the elementary, middle school, and high school levels with jobs encompassing being a general education teacher, a special education teacher, a reading specialist, and a principal designee. She is currently working as an associate professor at Southern New Hampshire University. She is passionate about working with prospective teachers. Her professional interests include teaching reading as well as working with special needs students and second-language learners. She is certified as a learning disabilities specialist (K–12), elementary educator (K–8), general special educator (K–12), and reading-writing specialist (K–12).

Marilyn Fenton, associate professor at Southern New Hampshire University, prepares her students to teach English language arts. She offers courses in the teaching of writing, methods of teaching (grades 5 to 12), and children's and adolescent literature. In the course of her earlier career teaching English in high schools in New York and New Hampshire, she taught students of all ability levels, including Advanced Placement classes in literature. As director of curriculum and instruction at a local high school, she supported competency-based instruction and smoother transitions among teachers of all subjects in the K–12 curriculum. Her special academic interests include the connection between reading and writing (grades 5 to 2). She received her BA in Russian language and Russian literature and her MA in foreign and comparative literature from the University of Rochester. She earned an EdD in curriculum and instruction from Argosy University (Sarasota, Florida).

Margaret Harris is a newly retired professor from Southern New Hampshire University, where she taught a number of courses primarily at the graduate level. Some of these courses in the School of Education were Content Literacy on Secondary Level, Social Studies Methods, The Educational Researcher, and the Student Teaching Seminar. She also taught one survey course in the School of Arts and Sciences in history, her content area. Prior to university teaching, she was assistant superintendent for curriculum and instruction for four years and a social studies teacher at the high school level for 27 years. She brings a plethora of experiences and years of service to education. She has her undergraduate degree in political science from the University of Massachusetts, Boston, and two master's degrees: one in liberal studies with an emphasis on Africa from Boston University and a master's in social science from Syracuse University. She completed her doctoral studies at the University of Massachusetts at Amherst.